Wh
What Others Are Saying

I would recommend *A Shattered Mind* to all therapists, teachers, and psychologists dealing with abused
children, as well as other survivors of childhood sexual
abuse. It is a powerful message of one woman's perse-
verance, with God's Love, to overcoming evil.

—Gary E. Warren, Ph.D

A Shattered Mind tugs at your very soul and is a must
read for therapists and counselors.

—Joseph R. Gianesin Ph.D. LICSW
Professor, Springfield College
School of Social Work

A SHATTERED MIND

DAUNA COLE

A SHATTERED MIND
ONE WOMAN'S STORY OF SURVIVAL AND HEALING

DAUNA COLE

TATE PUBLISHING *& Enterprises*

Published by Tate Publishing & Enterprises, LLC
127 E. Trade Center Terrace | Mustang, Oklahoma 73064 USA
1.888.361.9473 | www.tatepublishing.com

Tate Publishing is committed to excellence in the publishing industry. The company reflects the philosophy established by the founders, based on Psalm 68:11,
"The Lord gave the word and great was the company of those who published it."

Book design copyright © 2009 by Tate Publishing, LLC. All rights reserved.
Cover design by Cole Roberts
Interior design by Jeff Fisher

Published in the United States of America

ISBN: 978-1-61566-121-3
1. Psychology, Psychopathology, Dissociative Identity Disorder
2. Biography & Autobiography, Personal Memoirs
09.09.28

Acknowledgments

I want to thank my long-suffering husband, Robert, for always being there for me and supporting me and my alters over the last thirty-five years. I would not have survived without you.

To my daughters, Lorie and Christy, thank you for loving me no matter who I was at a given time. I love you both so dearly.

To Aimée Bradley, whose editing assistance helped me to turn my rambling journals into this book. To all of my therapists, psychologists, and psychiatrists, you've helped me to discover and heal myself and my alters. We all thank you.

Thank you to all of my friends who have supported me through this journey of self-discovery and healing.

Lastly, thank you Chuck and Millie Case, you are the parents I never had. You have loved and supported me through all of my highs and lows.

Table of Contents

Foreword

Foreword

Reading this book caused many emotions to stir inside of me. It made me want to believe the stories of abuse were not true. I have known the author for forty years. I met her when I was teaching a Hospital Services class to high school seniors. The first semester involved teaching the students skills to care for residents of a nursing home. The second semester the students were rotated in most areas of a hospital to expose them to areas the student might like to specialize in after high school. It was a very intense course. I could only accommodate twenty students in each of the three high schools where I taught the course. I had to be very selective and spent the first two to three weeks weeding out students that were not totally committed to the class. It was during this time of "deleting" students that Dauna arrived with a note from the principal of the high school saying, "This is Dauna. She would like to join your class. Would you consider accepting her in your class?" Though we were overcrowded, I felt I should give Dauna an opportunity. Her self-motivation, hard work-ethic, and keen mind impressed me. I enjoyed her very much as a student.

One day when we arrived at the nursing home, Dauna came without her uniform on. I was very upset because I had a patient assigned to her.

In a very angry tone, I asked, "Where is your uniform?" This did not phase her.

She said, "I need to talk to you!"

I said, "It better be important." Once I had the other students started with their assigned patients I returned to the conference room.

"Okay," I said. "What is it?"

Dauna said, "My baby boy was adopted out yesterday."

That did not shock me. This occurred quite often. So I asked her, "How old was he?" "Six months," she said. Since babies were usually snatched up when put up for adoption, her answer surprised me. "Why did it take so long?" I asked. What came next really shocked me! "He was my father's baby." That moment began a relationship between Dauna and me.

Over time parts of her story came out little by little. It made me feel sad, angry, and amazed. It caused unbelief and many other emotions. But I have always loved Dauna as a daughter.

I have prayed for her and experienced many of her joys, challenges and sorrows. But reading this book has given me a totally bigger picture of a real survivor of multifaceted abuse. There is a lot more that could be told that is not in this book. But Dauna has done a magnificent job of sharing her long journey through hell on earth, survival, and healing.

—Mildred Case,

Retired Nursing Instructor

Introduction

Introduction

In 1952, in rural California, I was born into a home with a pedophile father and a passive, codependent mother. Sexual abuse started when I was an infant and continued until I was sixteen, when I gave birth to my father's baby. As a result of the horrific abuse I suffered, my mind was shattered into many alternate personalities. Most of these personalities were formed when I was a child, and each held one or more memories of abuse.

Through this process, I was able to endure devastating abuse. In telling my story, I hope to share my difficult journey through childhood. I will talk about the people who abused me, the friends who made it bearable, and the people who have helped me survive. It has taken me a long time to uncover the extent of the abuse I endured. It was not always easy, but with God's help, I am on my way to recovery. Today, I live a normal life. Through sharing my struggle, I hope to help others who have suffered abuse in their childhood. Having a difficult childhood does not mean your adult life has to be ruined. With God, the help of others, and a positive attitude, it is possible to recover and break the cycle of addiction and abuse in your own life.

Chapter 1

Russian Roulette

The air was cool against my face as I walked the quarter mile from school to home. It was 1964, and I was in the seventh grade that year. The closer I got to home, the more my tranquility and freedom began to disappear.

Upon entering my house, I dropped my books onto the kitchen table, poured myself a glass of milk, and sat down to start my homework. Nobody was home yet. *Where is everyone?* I wondered. Suddenly Dad's red Studebaker truck sped into our driveway. In walked my dad. He got a beer from the fridge and came to the dining room where I sat. Grabbing me by the arm, he gruffly said, "C'mon, you're coming with me!" *Here we go again,* I thought. *What's it going to be tonight?*

We got into the truck and drove down the paved California road. It turned into a gravel road and headed toward Harper Lake. This was not an actual lake anymore but a dry lakebed in the middle of the

California desert. My dad smoked his nasty cigarettes and gulped down his beer as he drove, never saying one word to me. As evening came and the sun was getting low in the sky, we drove up to an old, abandoned, and fallen down house. There was a rickety barn next to the house. A windmill with a blade missing stood in the yard. Whenever the wind blew against the windmill, a clicking noise could be heard as it spun around and around.

Cars and trucks were parked outside of the old barn. We walked inside, and I could see bales of hay—straw really, at this point—scattered in one corner of the barn. Several men and teenage boys were hanging around smoking, drinking beer, and talking amongst themselves. Once we entered the barn, the talking stopped. All eyes turned toward my father and I. By the looks on their faces, it was as if the entertainment for the evening had just arrived.

In the center of the barn there was a broken stool with an old light bulb hanging from its electrical cord, just above the stool. It was the kind of light that a mechanic would use when they were working on cars. The electrical cord ran outside toward one of the trucks. I couldn't be sure from inside the barn, but I figured it must have been attached to the battery of one of the trucks parked outside. The light was shining toward the ground, casting light onto the broken stool.

My dad, gripping me by my elbow, pushed me in the direction of the stool. "You'll sit there," he said. When I looked around the barn, I could see the last remaining rays of the day's sun streaming through the spaces between the old boards that held the barn together. I could hear the wind blowing outside. Then the men and boys began to gather around me in a circle. Some were standing, some squatting, and some of the men were wearing uniforms. I guessed they must have been from the Air Force base where my dad worked.

My dad walked over to Al Anderson, one of his buddies, and handed him a large pistol. It had a long barrel. Dad took one bullet and put it in the chamber of the gun and spun the cartridge around.

He then stood over me with the gun and explained the game. "You have a choice. Have sex with each man here. If you refuse to have sex with any of them, we will put this gun to your head and pull the trigger."

I felt intense fear passing through me in a trembling fashion. My heart began to beat hard; I felt so scared! By that time, it had gotten dark in the barn. The only light was the hanging lamp that shone down on me as I sat on the stool in the center of the barn.

Al walked over to me and asked, "What's it going to be? Have sex with me, or have the trigger pulled?" I had heard of a strange game called Russian roulette somewhere before. *So this was what it was all about,* I thought. I looked at Al with his weathered, snake like skin, pointy cowboy boots, and his dirty jeans.

"No!" I said, defiantly. I heard the chamber spin. He held the barrel of the gun to my temple. I could feel the cold, hard metal against my skin. Al pulled the trigger. I heard a loud mechanical *click!* The chamber had been engaged, but there was no bullet this time. I felt somewhat relieved. I knew that I would be soon raped by these men and older boys, so I already felt like a part of me died. As I sat on the stool, the boys and the young soldiers came up to me one at a time. I couldn't tell you how many there were, just that the teen-aged boys had sex with me, but not the older men. They just watched the "show."

Sergeant John came up to me last. He was a huge black man with large, callused hands. How I hated him. I was left with Sergeant John the weekend before. He made me have sex with him that weekend, but that day on the stool was different. That day I would not let him rape me. I remembered thinking that I wished the gun would have already gone off, sending a bullet into my brain, then it would all have been over with. I'd never be raped, molested, beaten, or humiliated again. But no. The trigger was pulled, and the gun did not go off. It was finally over, and I was still alive. Sadness washed over me. All I had left was a letdown feeling. I had wished for freedom from this constant fear. I knew death would bring me freedom.

Driving home in the truck, the air was colder than when we had arrived at the barn. I sat in my seat trembling; I was cold, but also probably in shock. I was feeling so much despair. I felt dirty all over. My vagina stung a deep, aching hurt. The semen from so many men had soaked through my panties, and I cried quietly.

"Shut the hell up, you slut!" my father yelled. I tried to stop, but I began to sob, and the tears could not stop pouring down my face. From my face they ran down onto the front of my dress.

When we pulled into the driveway, it was late. I went inside to the bed I shared with my brother. Not even changing clothes, I just climbed onto my side of the bed and tried to go to sleep. I knew that come morning, I would have to go to school and act like nothing had happened the night before. I also knew that I was going to be in trouble again for not doing my homework. My teacher Mrs. Kreman would yell at me like usual. Crawling out of bed the next morning, I felt achy all over. I felt nasty and dirty, but because my brothers were already in the bathroom, I ended up just changing my clothes and making it to the table for breakfast. My mom never said a word about where I was the night before; she acted as if nothing had happened. So I said nothing, too, and life went on as usual.

Chapter 2

My Escapes

At age thirteen, my father gave me a buckskin quarter horse that I named Buck. Dad got the horse from a bucking string on a rodeo circuit. As generous as this gift may sound, Buck was only given to me as a form of blackmail. My father knew I would love this horse and told me that if I refused to have sex with him, he would give my horse away. Buck was my only way of escaping the chaos of home now and then. I did not attempt to ride Buck for a long time; he was just too wild. I would take him for long walks in the desert behind my house on a long lead rope. I would feed and brush him, and eventually he allowed me to ride him bareback. I could see Buck from my bedroom window. Sometimes in the middle of the night, I would go out to Buck's corral in my pajamas and brush and talk to him. He was my best friend.

I learned from experience that I could not ride Buck around a group of people, and I could not ride him with a saddle; he would revert back to his old rodeo days and would buck me off. Buck was an escape for me from the abuse of my home. He was my savior. I don't think I would have survived without him. Sometimes when I was being raped by my father or brother, I would allow my spirit to leave my body and travel out to where Buck was. My spirit would enter my horse and mingle with his. That allowed me to feel safe for a horrible time in my life.

Back at school, Mr. Stevens was one of my favorite teachers. He loved teaching, and we, in turn, really liked being his students. Unfortunately, I was not a good student. I had been under so much stress at home that I could not study my lessons. I had also missed so much school as a younger child that I did not have the basic skills of reading, writing, and math. When we had state testing, I did not read the questions; I just filled in the bubbles on the answer sheets so it would make an interesting design. Of course, since I never read the questions, I would score very low on my exams.

By the time I was preparing for high school, the elementary school principal thought I was "retarded," using that time period's terminology. The plan was to place me in special education classes when I entered high school. Before that happened, however, the principal had a school psychologist from San Bernardo come to our small elementary school in Hansonville, California, where I was given an IQ test. To everyone's surprise, I had an IQ of 148. Needless to say, I was placed in "regular" classes upon entering high school.

When I was fourteen, dad built a separate room behind the house; he called it the "Pool Room," complete with a pool table. This was the room that I slept in. Since my father and brother, Mike, came in constantly at night to have sex with me, I never felt safe there. Locking the door would get me in a lot of trouble. Dad and Mike would pound on the windows until I opened the door. Dad would then hit me once he was in the room. My father would rape me at least three times a week around three in the morning in that pool room. Mike would take the other one or two nights of the week to rape me.

My dad mixed with a group of pedophiles and would trade me to them for sex. This group included Sergeant John from the Air Force base; Al Anderson, my dad's friend; and a truck driver who lived in Lodi, California, with his wife and daughter. The truck driver would molest me and his own daughter while his wife watched. I would spend the weekend with them. The truck driver would come by my house in his big commercial truck and take me with him for the weekend. I also spent weekends with Sergeant John and Al Anderson, who also raped me.

My dad always smelled of body odor, cigarette smoke, and beer. He was never gentle or loving with me, always angry and rough. Each molestation would eventually lead to rape. Sometimes my father would sodomize me, and other times he would force me to perform oral sex. It is due to these childhood experiences that to this day I have a hard time brushing my teeth. I cannot sleep without a sheet or a blanket over me, and I still wake at three in the morning. Although much has improved, having sex with my husband is, understandably, sometimes very difficult.

Other memories of my father are that he was not circumcised. This is a fact no child should ever have to know. Dad always wore navy blue work pants and a T-shirt without any underwear when he came to rape me. His hands were rough and callused and were stained with nicotine from his cigarette smoking. On the weekends, sometimes dad would take me in his red pickup truck to drive along the railroad tracks, picking up wood that had fallen off the trains. It was really just an excuse, however, to rape me during the daytime on the weekends. I tried to escape, but it never worked. I hated this so much, and I hated my father even more. If I did not comply, he would pull his pistol out from behind the seat of his truck and threaten me with it.

I met a friend named Dan when I was fifteen. I thought he was a sweet, smart, and quiet boy. Even though he lived in the opposite direction from the bus stop, he would walk me home, carrying my books. I remember the one time he came to my house. He was sitting on my couch when my father came home. Dad threatened Dan and chased him out of the house. He told him to never return. My dad beat me for allowing him to come over. For our safety, we continued our very innocent relationship away from my home. We never even kissed. I didn't know that sex was meant to be between a husband and wife or boyfriends and girl-friends. I was groomed to believe that sex was some-thing evil that fathers, brothers, and strangers did to you. It was clearly *not* enjoyable to me. At times, my father would ask why I did not climax during sex. I did not have any idea what that meant. Obviously my father did not understand that rape and climax could never go hand-in-hand.

During this time in my life, I would walk alone to a church in Hansonville. I was given a white Bible and would sit on my bed and read it. I especially loved reading the New Testament. Reading the Bible helped me to keep my sanity intact during such a harsh time in my life. It gave me a sense of peace in my life. I started to pray to God and asked God to forgive me for my sins.

Another escape was the long rides I took on Buck to where my friend Carol lived. She lived on a ranch in Hansonville. This ranch was about five miles away, across the desert. On weekend and summer days, Carol and I would go riding together. We would ride bare back, and on the hottest days, we would ride the horses to her reservoir to cool us all off. What a wonderful and needed escape this was for me. When I was finally liberated from home, I had to leave Buck, and I knew I would probably never see him again. The last day I spent with him was so precious to me. I brushed him and talked to him about how sorry I was to leave him. I wished somehow I could take him with me, but that was just not possible. I don't really know what happened to Buck. I know my mom sold him to someone, but I have never seen him since. I know he would not be alive today, but I always wondered what happened to him. I felt like I abandoned him and still am brought to tears when I think about what he meant to me.

Chapter 3

Sixteen and Pregnant

Sixteen and Pregnant

When I was sixteen, I started my junior year of high school at Barlo High. I stopped having my periods sometime in September but hadn't really paid much attention to what was going on with my cycles. By Halloween, I had gone to a parade in Barlo, California, with Dan. He was working at a dairy then and had just bought himself a new Camaro. At the parade, I started feeling like I was going to faint. I was dizzy and nauseous, so Dan took me home. I went straight to bed and to my disappointment did not feel any better in the morning. I returned to school after a few days and was taking a history test when I suddenly vomited all over my desk. After some time had passed, I began to suspect I was pregnant. Since I had never been sexual with Dan, I knew I was not pregnant by him. It had to be my father or brother's child. It was also possible that I was pregnant by one of the other men my father had traded me for sex.

After I was certain I was pregnant, I mustered the

courage and told my dad; I was so scared. I remember that we were standing out in the back yard when I finally got up my nerve to tell him.

He spat at me, "Don't you ever tell anyone that you are pregnant, or I will take you out into the desert and shoot you right in the head! No one will ever find your body."

His words chilled me to the bone. I didn't know what I was going to do. I did know that my father had access to many guns and that he would not hesitate to kill me. I was never called Dauna by him, just "bitch," "slut," and "whore." My father hated me as much as I hated him. To him, I was just an object to have sex with and then throw away.

I finally told Dan what was happening to me, and he told his mother. She had the police come to her house to talk to me, and they made a report. I was with Dan at his house when the police questioned me. I finally told them about what had been happening with my father, my brother, and the other men. I can remember Dan's mom asking me, "What do you think of your father *now?*" I thought that was a strange question because I had *always* hated my father. The police did nothing. They did not arrest my father, nor did they remove me from my home. I was so devastated.

Dan was so sweet. He told me, "Let's get married, and I will raise this baby as my own." I did love Dan, but I did not want to get married and live in Barlo with a kid at age sixteen. I decided it was time to tell my mother I was pregnant. She was very angry, and of course, blamed everything on me. I told her I thought Dad was the father of the baby. Even though she had to have known my father had been molesting me since I was three years old, she continued to blame the pregnancy on my relationship with Dan. In the meantime, Dan had given me an engagement ring and proposed marriage. I did accept the ring but did not make a commitment about marriage. My parents wanted to drive us to Kingman, Arizona, to get married, but I refused.

Abortion was legal in 1968 for incest cases, so my mother asked me if I wanted to have one. I knew that if I had an abortion, I would not be able to leave my abusive home life behind me. I didn't want an abortion. I just wanted to get away from all of the abuse I had been surviving for so long. My mother's reaction was to forbid me from telling anyone else that Dad was the father of the baby. Instead, she had a social worker from the county come to the house. My mom told the social worker I was pregnant with Dan's baby. They decided to place me in a maternity home for unwed mothers in San Bernardo, California. At last, I was finally leaving the abuse behind me. I was so happy.

The county sent me to the Puddy home in San Bernardo. Olive and Jack Puddy were a nice, older, English couple. There were about ten other pregnant girls living in the Puddy home. The weather that year was unseasonably rainy; the gray weather matched my mood. For school, I was placed at the Cottage School for Unwed Mothers, where I was treated like a slut for being an unwed, pregnant teenager. The stigma was horrible then.

Dan visited me when he could, which helped elevate my mood some. By this time, he had been thrown out of the house by his mother and stepfather. Dan moved to a nearby town to live and also continued to work at the dairy. He did this all while attending his

senior year at Barlo High School. Dan received a com-
mission to the Naval Academy, but he did not want
to go. He still hoped I would marry him. I insisted
that Dan go, and although he did end up going to
the Naval Academy, he hated it there and quit after
a few months. This meant, however, that Dan was
forced to go fight in Vietnam. I have never seen him
since. I heard over the years that he married a women
from Vietnam and they had a couple kids. I cared a
lot about Dan and would have loved to see him again.

I saw a social worker once a week while I lived in
the Puddy home. It was in the spring of 1969 that I
realized the social worker thought the baby would be
born with brown hair and eyes like Dan. I knew this
was not going to be the case, however. I knew this
child would be born with blonde hair and green or
blue eyes like my dad and I. Not wanting the child to
be placed in the wrong home, I finally told the social
worker that my dad was the father of my baby. The
social worker reported this to the police in San Bernardo. After finishing school one afternoon, I got onto
the bus to go back to the Puddy home. I never made
it back, as a policeman came right onto my school bus
and took me off of it. I ended up at the police station,
sitting in a chair under a large, round spotlight, just
like you see in the movies. I was interrogated there
for hours.

At the police station, the officers kept asking me
the same questions over and over. This ordeal would
have tired anyone, but being very pregnant by that
time, I was utterly exhausted. I finally said, "Look,
either you let me go now, or I will change my story
and say that none of this is true." I was finally taken
back to the Puddy home. The next day, my father was

arrested by the U.S. Air Force Police, the San Bernardo Police, and the Kern County Police. What a scene that must have been.

Late in my pregnancy, I developed preeclampsia, where my blood pressure was very high. I was admitted to the hospital so I could receive treatment for the elevated blood pressure. I felt awful, both physically and mentally. I stayed in the hospital for about one week before I was released back to the Puddy home.

When my brothers came to visit me, I thought they had come because they cared about me and my condition, but I couldn't have been more wrong. They came to convince me to drop the charges against dad. This was such an upsetting visit that my blood pressure ended up being elevated once again. In the end, I told the police I was not well enough to testify against my father. I did not understand that I would not be required to testify right away, and it would take months or years before this ever got to court. This was never explained to me. My father ended up being released from jail, and he immediately left the state.

During this very upsetting ordeal, I had to be readmitted to the hospital. I ended up going into labor. My mother was called to come to be with me at the hospital. She may as well have been a stone, for she did not support me in any way throughout my labor. My mother sat beside my bed in a chair and acted like I was "the other woman." Mom did not care about me in any way, shape, or form. Her only concern was about my dad. In the early morning hours on May 24, 1969, when I gave birth to a nine-pound, eight-ounce baby boy, all my mother did was run to the nursery to see if he really was her husband's. The baby was blonde with greenish-blue eyes, just like my father's.

After giving birth, all I wanted to do was hold my baby just one time before I had to give him up for adoption, but the nurses said, "No!" This was so upsetting to me that I ended up with full-blown eclampsia and had a seizure. After treating my seizure, the nurses gave me my son to hold. I remember him being such a big baby. He was almost bald with blonde fuzz on top of his head. What a fat baby he was, too, with rolls of fat on his arms and legs. How I wished that I could keep him, but I knew I would not be able to care for him properly. My son was taken to a foster home for six months where he was given a battery of tests to make sure he was normal, due to being fathered by his own grandfather.

I recovered from the pregnancy and delivery and returned to living with Jack and Olive Puddy. They were fine people. I found it difficult watching the pregnant girls come into the Puddy home, give birth, and then return home. This caused me to relive my ordeal over and over again.

In September of 1969, I returned to high school for my last year. I was a senior at last. I decided I wanted to take a nurses aid course that was being offered at San Bernardo High School. The class was so full that the teacher had to eliminate five students who had already enrolled in the class, but I was determined to get in. At this same time, our high school was being renovated, so the school was using a temporary building. I remember the principal didn't even have an office of his own. His desk was in a corner of a larger room without even a curtain separating him from the rest of the administration and registration desks. I went to him and told him I wanted to be in the nurses aid class. His reply was, "No, it's too full."

I decided I would not accept that answer, so I sat in a chair near the principal's area and stared at him all day for two days. He must have finally gotten sick of seeing me because he gave me a note to take to Millie Case, the nursing instructor. The note read, "This is Dauna; she would like to join your class. Would you consider accepting her into your class?" With much excitement, I took the note to the teacher. Millie Case was horrified at the prospect of having one more student. She felt obligated to give me a chance anyway and told me that if I passed all of the basic nursing skills, she would keep me in her class. I was already two weeks behind everyone else, so I remember having to work very hard to catch up. I ended up being the first student to complete all of the basic nursing skills, so I was allowed to stay. Millie Case and I are close friends to this day.

During class, we would change our clothes and put on our nurses aid uniforms. We would go by bus to a convalescent home where we first learned to care for patients. Our class had been moved to a new school, which I believe was called Canyon High School. During this time, there was rioting between the black students and everyone else at our high school. The building we were in had no windows and had tall cement and wrought iron walls around it. It looked and felt like a prison.

We were dropped off in front of those walls around noon every day where we'd have to go to the nursing classroom to change out of our uniforms. For several days there were riot police surrounding the school, and groups of rioting black students were roaming around our campus. Police were shooting tear gas in order to break up the crowds. This is what we had to run through to get to our classrooms. We banged on the door to be let in (remember there were no windows). The teacher did not know who was pounding on her door, so she did not open it. After about ten minutes of pounding and screaming, we were at last let in. This happened two days in a row. It was a turbulent time and place to be a student.

After the pregnancy, I had horrible stretch marks on my abdomen. I was so embarrassed in our PE class and did not want the other girls to see me naked in the shower. I did not want them to know I had had a baby. I told the PE teacher that I could not shower with the other girls because I had bad cramps from being chilled. I even brought a note from my doctor. The gym teacher was very mean to me, however, and made fun of me in front of the other girls. They all hated me because of that. The teacher made me wear ugly white sweatpants and a sweatshirt instead of dressing out and showering. The girls still teased me for that, but at least I didn't have to shower. How I hated PE that year!

Toward the end of my senior year, I had driver's education with Mr. Rigoly. He was also my high school guidance counselor. My driving class was a few times a week. One day he had planned to drive me home last, after dropping off the other students first. I thought nothing of this. Nothing, that is, until we parked near the Puddy home and Mr. Rigoly leaned over across the seat and kissed me as I started to leave the car. I was shocked and scared. I reported this to my nursing instructor. She, in turn, reported this incident to the principal. I was disgusted, however, when the principal did nothing about it—ever. I had to see this man's face until the end of that year when I finally graduated. This, of course, would bring to mind the abuse from my father. I have regretted many times between then and now that I never testified against my father. I remain so very angry that he was able to rape, molest, and terrorize me for all of those years, only to get away with it.

In November, 1969, I was taken to the County Child Protective Services building and asked to sign adoption papers, giving up my son. He was six months old at that time and given a clean bill of health. I cried when I saw him and cried more when I signed the papers, but I wanted him to have two loving parents who would give him a stable home. I knew I could not provide this for him; so in a pain-filled act of love, I signed the papers, hoping I was giving him a better life, and left the building.

Chapter 4

Falling in Love

In June of 1970, I graduated from San Bernardo High School. My grades had gone from D's and F's back at home, to all A's at San Bernardo High. I even completed my Nurse's Aide Certification. I moved into the foster home of Dr. Kern and Jane Pihl, and I started to feel that I could turn my life around.

Living with the Pihls, I had opportunities to get in touch with my spirituality and eventually was baptized into the Seventh Day Adventist Church. Millie Case, my nurse's aide instructor from high school, helped me to apply for and receive my letter of acceptance at Loma Linda University, La Sierra Campus, to study pre-nursing. I was even given a scholarship, a grant, and a loan! This scholastic support was such a motivator for me. I also worked in the school kitchen, preparing salads, desserts, and serving meals. I found my classes to be extremely challenging, especially the anatomy and physiology class. It was because of this difficult class that I needed a tutor. I met a sweet, quiet boy in my class named Robert Cole. Robert tutored me in that subject.

I lived in the college dorm and loved it. My two roommates were Jane and Sheri. We loved being together, and in spite of the many rules to follow, we always had so much fun. When other dorm-dwellers may have complained about the early seven o'clock curfew, Jane, Sheri, and I felt like we were having a constant slumber party. I think that our roommate fun was a very needed balance to the hard work I was doing. Due to studying diligently, working in the school kitchen, and other life stressors, I would often get migraine headaches that were almost unbearable. I didn't realize it at the time, but thinking about my son constantly was also the source of a deep depression. I would later learn that this was how my alter George came to be; he was there to study for me.

I was nineteen during the summer that followed my freshman year. I moved back in with the Pihl family while I worked as a nurses aide at Loma Linda Medical Center. My freshman roommate, Jane, moved in with me and worked as a cashier at the hospital's cafeteria. Because I worked the three to eleven shift, Jane and I saw each other coming and going. Most of my shift was spent on the oncology ward. I loved my patients and always gave them lots of my "TLC," but it was so very hard to watch them die on a daily basis.

My former tutor, Robert Cole, was now a student on the Loma Linda University campus, studying medical technology. We ended up rekindling our budding relationship and falling in love with each other. Robert would walk me home at midnight after my shift was done each night.

Because I ended up having to drop my anatomy

and physiology class in my freshman year, I was not able to continue with my Bachelor of Science degree in RN studies. When I returned to La Sierra campus, I started the associate degree nursing course instead.

It was 1971 by this time, and although I studied hard, my heart was not in my studies. My depression was left unchecked, which caused me to become profoundly suicidal. I remember seeing a doctorate candidate student counselor named Tom. He tried his best to help me, but I was beyond his capabilities.

I eventually left school and returned to Loma Linda where Robert lived. I rented a room with the Gurney family, just across the street from the hospital; this also meant that Robert and I could spend as much time as possible together. Before we became engaged, I told him all about my past abuse. Robert was so understanding and supportive of me; to say I was relieved would have been a huge understatement. When I went with Robert to meet his family in Palm Springs, I was so afraid they would not like me. I need not have worried, however, because they were nice to me. I ended up liking them a lot.

Eventually, I decided I needed to try having a sexual relationship with Robert because I was worried I would not be able to have one with him after we married. It was perhaps the pressure I was putting myself under to have sex with Robert that caused a terrible migraine headache that same day. Robert placed a cool cloth on my forehead. He began to soothe me by stroking my hair. Looking back on this evening, it was no surprise to me that we made love for the first time in the wee hours that followed Robert's tender loving care. Sex was not like anything I had ever experienced; I realized this is what it felt like to be intimate with someone you loved. He was so gentle with me. I never knew how special making love could be.

Robert and I were married in Mathisen Chapel on the La Sierra campus on June 16, 1972. I was twenty years old. Robert had graduated just five days prior and was ready to do a year of interning at the Loma Linda University Medical Center's lab. Barely able to afford our wedding, we were not able to give ourselves a honeymoon. Although we used borrowed flowers and were not able to hire a photographer, I have such fond memories of our wedding. It was so special to me that I remember it like it was yesterday. Robert, being the great guy he was (and still is), bought me the dress I had been dreaming of. The bridesmaids wore long gowns in pastel colors: pink, yellow, purple, and blue, made with dotted Swiss fabric. Each brides-maid carried a single rose that matched the color of her gown. Each rose had a coordinating ribbon, which wrapped around the rose, ending in steamers hanging down. I carried a beautiful bouquet of red roses, while the men in the wedding party all wore rose bouton-nieres in their white dress jackets. My friend, Carol, sang with guitar accompaniment. She sang, "The First Time Ever I Saw Your Face" and "You Needed Me."

The first night Robert and I spent as husband and wife was an adventure; we ended up breaking the bed. I felt so comfortable being with Robert that being intimate was no longer an issue. Later the next day, it was time to visit family as the new Mr. and Mrs. Cole. First we went to see Robert's mother, sisters, and brother in Palm Springs for a night; then we drove to Barlo the following day to visit my mother and broth-ers, but that evening was spent at a crummy motel in

Victorville on an ice-cold water bed. That night was a disaster.

We initially lived in a small house in San Bernardo. Eventually, we moved to a two bedroom apartment, which was part of an old Victorian house in Loma Linda. I worked at Loma Linda University Hospital (LLU); this is also where Robert was finishing his internship. We were poor but happy. Robert got a stipend of $250.00 a month, and not surprisingly, I made very little as a nurse aide.

Chapter 5

Becoming a Mother

Becoming a Mother

I became pregnant while working at the LLU Medical Center. I was exhausted, nauseated, and spotting heavily. My OB doctor warned me that the spotting indicated I could lose the baby. Working in this condition began to take a heavy toll on me. At the end of my shift, I could barely crawl up the steps to my apartment. The doctor felt the pregnancy was in the process of aborting itself and said that it most likely had something very wrong with it. My bleeding became heavier, and it was then that Robert and I decided to abort the baby. I remember driving to the Community Hospital in Riverside and spending a night there. The abortion happened the following day. Although we felt badly that this little life was not meant to be, I have never regretted our decision; it was a decision we made together, and it was for the best in the long run.

Robert finished his internship in June of 1973, and he took a job at Barlo Community Hospital. The last place I wanted to go was back to Barlo, but we did just the same. I also worked at the same hospital as an aide. We stayed with my mother while searching for an apartment. Robert and I both hated it there. We lasted two weeks, quit our jobs and moved to Hemet. Robert got a good job in the hospital there, and I started school at San Gorgonio College.

While studying early childhood education at San Gorgonio College, we became pregnant again. This pregnancy felt totally different. I felt good and had no spotting whatsoever. Robert and I took the prepared childbirth classes, and I started going to the La Leche League to learn about breast-feeding our baby. I read any book I could get my hands on that had to do with childbirth, childhood growth and development, and parenting. I remember feeling so much healthier. I rode my men's twelve-speed bike all over Hemet, even when my belly got to be so big that it looked like I was riding with a basketball under my shirt.

On May 11, 1974, my water broke, and following a natural, non-medicated labor, Lorie Ann Cole was born. She weighed in at seven pounds, nine ounces, and was twenty-two-inches long. Lorie turned out to be a crier. She cried from birth on! She cried and cried and cried. No one could calm her except her daddy. Robert would hold her, and she'd quiet down immediately, falling right to sleep. I was so relieved when she would finally stop crying. I was also happy that Robert could calm her. On the other hand, I was just a little bit jealous. I also wanted that effect on my daughter.

When Lorie was just six months old, we moved to Palm Springs, where Robert got a job at a reference lab in Palm Desert. We bought our very first house there. I loved being a mom; Lorie made it easy as she got a bit older. She was such a bright and creative child. I was twenty-three when I started taking classes at the College of the Desert, where I continued my studies in early childhood education. My mother-in-law, Lorene, would watch Lorie while I took just one or two classes at a time. Lorie and I participated in some Mommy and Me classes, swimming classes, and eventually, a parent-cooperative preschool. I completed my associates degree when Lorie was about a year old.

Life was moving along pretty well at that time, and Robert and I decided to have a second child. I had my IUD removed and became pregnant within a month. This pregnancy, too, was easy and uneventful. Because my own maternal instincts had kicked in, I was trying to have a relationship with my mother, but that proved to be very difficult. Being a mother myself, I still had such anger that my own mother had not protected me against my father's abuse and that she always sided with my father, making me the culprit.

By December of 1977, I was getting so tired of being pregnant. At last, I went into labor. I arrived at the local hospital around nine p.m. Labor was heating up, but the doctor had not yet arrived. My nurse put me on a gurney and pushed it just inside of the delivery room door. She warned, "Don't push!" I was using the Lamaze method of childbirth, so I was panting and blowing like crazy to keep from pushing. Christy was born before midnight on December 21, 1977, while I was still on that gurney. By the second evening of her life, Christy began sleeping through the night; needless to say, she was a very easy baby. Big sister Lorie, however, had some adjusting to do; she was not entirely thrilled to have a baby sister at first.

Anxious for more space for our growing family, we sold our house in Palm Desert and had our new home built in Cathedral City. In the meantime, we moved in with Robert's mother, sister, and her family. To say that we were cramped was an understatement. Since we were only expected to be there a couple of months, it felt doable. Unfortunately, we ended up staying four and a half months longer than expected as we waited for the house to finish.

When we finally were able to move into the house, it was quickly apparent that our new, spacious home was well worth the wait. The children enjoyed a much larger, fenced yard to play in, and Robert and I enjoyed putting in the landscaping, sprinkler system, and spa.

It was at this time, however, that I also began having a problem with a major depression episode. Although I always tried to keep my girls from knowing what I was experiencing, I couldn't help but wonder if they could sense a shift in their mommy. My sex life was nonexistent, and I started having nightmares. Thus began my visit to the first in a long line of therapists. Licensed Clinical Social Worker, John Shaeffer, was my first real therapist. Although he was said to specialize in work with incest survivors, I never felt that he was very sensitive to my feelings. I tried to work with him for about six months, but in the end I gave up.

That September, Lorie was in kindergarten. I attended the College of the Desert, where I took my prerequisite classes for their nursing program. By this time, I was feeling a bit better and had become Lorie's kindergarten "room mother." I was also active in the school's parent-teacher group.

Because I spent a great deal of time with Lorie before school started—helping her learn her letters, numbers, and colors—and because she could already read upon entering kindergarten, her teacher had her IQ tested. They found that she had an elevated IQ and felt she could be moved up to the first grade. After a lengthy meeting with the school psychologist, the principal, Lorie's teacher, and Robert and I, it was decided to move Lorie to first grade so she would not be bored in kindergarten.

I began helping other parents at Lorie's school with fundraisers and painting over graffiti on the walls with murals. I also became a Brownie leader for Lorie. For Christy, who desperately wanted more than anything to get involved like her big sister, I started a mini-scouts group for the preschool sisters of the Brownies. I even made their outfits. Both girls were doing well in their schools, but all was not well with Robert and I at that time. We had begun fighting; Robert was not at all interested in parenting the girls. Since he felt this was a woman's job, he left it all up to me. With my background of abuse, I had never had a positive role model for parenting. The fundamentals of having a good marriage were also a mystery to me. I read self-help books on parenting and marriage to improve my skills. Parenting classes were also an invaluable resource.

Little Christy was becoming a very angry toddler and preschooler. She had terrible tantrums and destroyed Lorie's things. I tried using the time-out method and distracting her, but nothing seemed to help. Recognizing we all needed help, I started seeing a very caring and compassionate therapist named Sandy Holmes. She helped us a great deal with our parenting and marriage issues. With these new skills, it got easier to parent Christy, and life in our household became much happier.

I was finally was able to start in the nursing program at the local junior college and enrolled Christy in a cooperative preschool where parent participation was involved. Christy ended up not liking it because she was already reading and writing, and like her big sister, she, too, already knew her numbers, colors, shapes, and her letters. I had a kindergarten teacher test her and found that she was ready for kindergarten, even though she was only four years old. She started that fall. Christy loved kindergarten; she excelled to the point of reading the most books in her class that year.

Chapter 6

Memories Begin Coming Back

Sadie's Story

Sadie's Story

My family life seemed to be improving and my career was getting back on track when I had the first of many setbacks. Around four a.m. the night before we were planning to leave on a family vacation, a memory of a ten-year-old girl emerged to Robert. I did not recall telling him, but Robert told me I had woken up with a start and said my name was Sadie. I told him I had been running. My gown was wet with sweat, as if I had been running in my sleep. At the time, I did not understand what happened. It seemed more like sleepwalking or a bad nightmare than a memory of something that I had actually experienced. Here is Sadie's story.

Sometimes in the summer, my family would take a trip to northern California. We would go camping at a campground overlooking the ocean. I usually loved these trips, but not that year. I had gone for a walk in the big pine trees near the campground. My dad came up from behind me and said, "Get back to camp; you're not supposed to be out here alone." I ran through the forest back toward our camp. My dad was following me. I reached the camp, and no one was there; my mom and brothers had gone down to the beach. Soon after I got back to camp, my father arrived there too. My dad forced me into the tent. The sleeping bags were laid out on the floor of the tent. He forced me onto the sleeping bag on the floor, just in front of the zippered opening of the tent. He raped me as he had done so many times before. I could hardly breathe with his full weight on top of me. His chest was pressing against my face. I could smell his body odor. I felt like I was going to vomit.

The following day, I was in the tent reading a book. My dad came into the tent. I thought I was safe because my mother was sitting near the camp fire just outside of the tent. My father put his hand over my mouth and whispered in my ear, "Don't make a sound." I knew what was coming, and I was right, of course. My dad raped me right there and then. When he finished his dirty business with me, he walked out of the tent and sat down next to my mom by the fire. I felt so dirty and violated. I began to wonder what I had done to cause this abuse. I thought it must be my fault. I wondered if this was happening to the other girls I knew at school. None of them had ever talked to me about it. Maybe I was just such a bad girl that I was being punished.

Chapter 7

Nursing School

Nursing School

In 1982, I was in my third semester of nursing school, and we were about to study psychology. This study included a rotation at Patton State Psychiatric Hospital. I was very worried that I would have to go to the Mentally Disordered Sex Offenders locked unit at the hospital, so I shared this with Sandy, my therapist. It was her suggestion that I take my concerns to the director and nursing school instructors. I explained my background of abuse as much as was needed and indicated that I'd like to be sent to a different unit in the hospital. Unfortunately for me, the outcome of my plea was not going to go the way I needed it to go. It was decided that I should be sent to the very unit I was so terrified of in order to face the issues and fears in my life. I was very upset.

I went to the Mentally Disordered Sex Offenders unit twice a week for one month. I was so terrified of the men on that unit. I had to attend their group meetings and listen to them discuss their crimes against women and children. Most of the men said they were not to blame for their crimes but blamed the victims instead. This experience sent me into another major depression. This time I received the help of a psychiatrist and began taking medication for my depression. I had horrible nightmares, which caused me to have trouble sleeping. Sandy started doing hypnotherapy with me, where many memories surfaced under hypnosis that I could not face in my conscious state. These were memories of the sexual abuse at the hands of my father, brothers, and my father's friends. I would see Sandy once a week. These frightening memories would emerge, and then the session would end, and it was time to go. I was not sure if these memories were real or not, but they felt real, and I was scared and confused. Instead of helping me to address these memories, I was left on my own to try and deal with them by myself for a week, until the next session. I kept plunging deeper into depression and soon became suicidal.

It was at that point that I cut off my relationship with my mother and brothers. I finally could see that my mother had to have known about the abuse my father inflicted upon me and just chose to ignore it. She never acknowledged my abuse or even said she was sorry that I went through such hell as a child.

Around this time, I was also finding it hard to continue on in the nursing program. Just when I thought I couldn't go on another day, my fourth semester started, and we rotated to intensive care where God sent me a wonderful and supportive instructor. She was the only reason I was able to finish my nursing program at all. In June of 1983, I graduated. I couldn't have been more proud of myself! I sat for my state board examination that summer in Pasadena, California.

The exams lasted two days, and I remember them being very hard. In August, when I thought I couldn't stand to wait another second, I received my state board results in the mail. I had passed the boards! I was now a registered nurse. Not only had I passed my examination, I scored a 2468; the minimum score needed to pass was 1600. Thinking back to when my principal thought I was retarded, I smiled a wide, satisfied grin. God had guided me through nursing school.

Although I wanted to work in the labor and delivery unit in the hospital, I knew that this would require working the night shift. With Robert working the night shift, I would not have anyone available to stay with and care for the girls, so I took a job caring for an elderly lady named Mary Mackey. Although I started out caring for her in the afternoons, I was eventually needed to care for her during the daytime. This worked well, as I would drive the girls to school, go to work during the day, and be home with them in the afternoon.

Christy was six then; Lorie was nine. Both girls continued to love school. They both played soccer and were still involved in Girl Scouts. I was still enjoying being their "room mother" in each of their classrooms. As smooth as things looked on the surface, they were turbulent just beneath. Christy was having more angry outbursts, and she and Lorie hated one another. Robert and I were not doing well in our marriage. He would not talk with me about his feelings and still refused to help parent our daughters. I was contemplating a divorce.

Things continued on this way for several years. The girls were growing up before my eyes. I was finally getting to the point where I was feeling better emotionally and no longer attended therapy, although I did attend a ninety-minute weekly support group called Women Molested As Children. I continued caring for Mrs. Mackey, and by now she was getting senile. She would constantly believe that people were stealing from her. I can't even remember the hundreds of times we had to count her silver to prove it was all still there.

Chapter 8

Joe's Memory

Joe's Memory

Without warning, another memory came back to me in the middle of the night. This time, it was a young boy named Joe who came forward. Here is Joe's story.

In the summer when I was eight, I had been playing in the back yard without my shoes. I hated shoes and only wore them when I was forced to. My dad and his friend, Mr. Anderson, approached me and asked, "Do you want to come with us and play a game?" This sounded like it might be fun, so I said, "Okay," and climbed into Mr. Anderson's truck. After I climbed in the front seat, sitting between Mr. Anderson and my dad, I felt a twinge of fear shoot through me. *Maybe this was not such a good idea after all*, I thought.

We drove a few miles to Mr. Anderson's house. We walked to the back of the old ranch house where the chicken coop was. I spent some time chasing the chickens around the chicken coop, not really paying any attention to my dad and Mr. Anderson. They had gone inside for a while. Sitting around the backyard alone, a short time later, I saw several wire chicken cages. Each cage was about one yard by one yard with a wire top that opened and closed. These cages were empty. I thought nothing of that, but later I would see what they would be used for.

Mr. Anderson came to me first and said, "I will tell you how we play this game." I had forgotten all about the game we had come to play. Mr. Anderson unzipped his pants, and exposed himself. I tried to run back to the old ranch house to hide. The back door was locked, so I started to run to the front door. Just as I was about to round the corner of the house, my dad grabbed me.

He said, "Come on, we just want to play a game with you." He held my arm tight in his grip. He dragged me across the backyard toward the coop. I was terrified.

My dad pulled my shorts off with one hand, while holding on to me with the other.

Mr. Anderson approached me and commanded, "You climb up on that bale of hay."

I complied, not because I wanted to, but because I knew that I had no choice. Mr. Anderson tried to force himself on me. He did not succeed because I was squirming away from him.

My dad said, "Okay, if that's the way you want to play this game, that's fine by us." Mr. Anderson opened the top of one of the chicken cages and forced me into it, closing the top with a "clap."

"Let's see how you like being in there for an hour or so," he said.

My dad and Mr. Anderson went back in the house. It was a hot summer day, and I was naked in the small cage. I was all rolled up in a ball, crying quietly. I did not want to make them angrier at me. I was so hot and scared. I wondered how I was going to get away. I tried to push open the top of the cage, but it would not budge.

After an hour had passed that felt more like three hours, my dad and Mr. Anderson came out of the house. Mr. Anderson was holding something that looked like a stick.

"Are you ready to play the game?" Mr. Anderson said.

I said, "No, just let me out of here and take me home."

Suddenly, Mr. Anderson pushed that stick through the cage and shocked me on my bare bottom. I guess what he was holding was a cattle prod. I screamed out with pain.

"Well, are you ready to play now?" Mr. Anderson said. He ended up shocking me two more times before I finally complied. I had no way of getting away or stopping them.

I was sodomized that day by both of them. The pain was excruciating and blood came from my rectum. After they were finished with me, my dad forced me to put on my shorts and get in the truck for the ride home. I could barely walk, and climbing into the truck was difficult. Sitting was impossible. My dad pushed me from behind yelling, "Get the hell up there." He said, "Shut the hell up, you baby you." I was taken home. I was crying and bleeding, but Mom said nothing to me about what had happened or where I had been.

Chapter 9

Brain Surgery

Brain Surgery

Toward the end of 1985, I began to feel very ill, with headaches, nausea, dizziness, and constant fatigue. I saw a neurologist in December, and a CAT scan was ordered. The results came back with a diagnosis of Communicating Hydrocephalus[1]. I was admitted to a renown teaching hospital, a moderate drive from our home, where many tests were taken. One of the tests I remember was taken on the Nuclear Medicine unit. A special radioactive dye was inserted into my spinal canal, which was supposed to travel to my brain so pictures of my brain could be taken. The radiology results showed that none of the dye traveled to my brain, it remained only in my spinal canal, which would indicate a blockage. These findings were not addressed by the doctor, however. Based on the results of the CAT scan taken earlier, I was taken into surgery.

Once in surgery, a Lumbar Peritoneal Shunt was placed internally from my spinal canal to my abdomen. I was in the hospital for a few days when, just before being discharged, I noticed a swollen lump at both my spinal and abdominal shunt sites. I told this to the resident physician as he was writing my discharge orders. My concerns were minimized, and I was sent home.

After several days at home, the swollen areas had increased in size, as did my headaches, dizziness, and nausea. This was very frightening to me. I began to feel very ill. Robert returned me to the hospital where I had to sit in the emergency room for hours before someone from the Neurology unit came to examine me. By this time, I was so ill that I could not even stand up on my own.

The resident physician in the emergency room ordered another CAT scan, which showed a possible tumor in my brain. This had not been seen before. The radiologist called my neurosurgeon and told him to do no more surgeries until an MRI was done, but my neurosurgeon ignored this request. Apparently, the neurosurgeon knew my shunt had slipped prior to releasing me from the hospital; the lumps at both ends of the shunt were symptoms of the slippage, but he did nothing about it. Ignoring the radiologists request to hold off further surgeries until an MRI could be completed, the neurosurgeon decided to reposition the Lumbar Peritoneal Shunt in my spinal canal. He took me back into surgery immediately.

On top of everything else that had gone wrong at this hospital, just before a urinary catheter was placed into my bladder, it was dropped onto my bed, which compromised the sterile field. As a result of the carelessness, I contracted a bladder infection. When I told my doctor that I had a bladder infection, a culture was ordered, which came back "positive." Although the culture's findings were placed onto my chart, no actions was taken to treat the infection. When it was decided that I could be released from the hospital some days later, I again asked about my urine culture results and was told, "You have a bladder infection." I was sent home with a prescription for antibiotics. I was so thankful to get out of the hospital before anything else went wrong!

I was very sick when I got home and only became sicker. I could not sit up or walk, nor could I care for my children. When I eventually fell asleep, I would stop breathing. When I had been home less than a week, my sister-in-law came over to check on me. The next thing I knew, she had me on a rolling chair and pushed me out to the car. She drove me to the local hospital emergency room. My sister-in-law had called a friend, a neurosurgeon named Dr. John Thompson. She contacted him prior to our arrival at the hospital. Once in the emergency room, Dr. Thompson ordered an emergency CAT scan, which showed that I did not have Communicating Hydrocephalus at all; I had a tumor in my brain and Obstructive Hydrocephalus[2]. The treatment I had received at the first hospital had only made me more sick.

Dr. Thompson immediately took me into surgery. Once in surgery, he placed a drain from my ventricles to relieve the pressure in my brain, which then drained the excess fluid into sterile drainage bottles. After three days in the neurosurgery ward, I had to be taken back to the operating room for a tedious eight-hour surgery. I was in a coma in intensive care for one week, and my condition continued to decline. Once again, I needed to be taken back into surgery; this time Dr. Thompson was looking for a blood clot on my brain.

He was looking for anything to explain my worsening condition. He called my former doctor, the surgeon who performed the original surgery, three times and got no response. Dr. Thompson finally gave up and opened up my spine; out popped the shunt that had been left in place so many weeks prior. I was returned to intensive care and ended up staying in the hospital for several more weeks. With my medical problem finally solved, I gradually recovered enough to be sent home.

Once home, the recovery was a long one. I found it hard to care for my daughters; I was unable to drive again for some time for fear of having a seizure while driving. My reading and short-term memory abilities were affected due to the swelling in my brain. On a positive note, I was alive! The mass in my brain turned out to be a benign cyst. Though it would grow back slowly over many years, I would not need chemotherapy or radiation. It was time to start my life all over again.

Chapter 10

Lost Time and Voices

Lost Time and Voices

In the late eighties, after having recovered from my illness, I took a job caring for a twenty-three-year-old girl named Stella. Stella had been injured in a car accident when she was fifteen years old and was a non-speaking quadriplegic as a result of her accident. I came to love Stella, and when she would smile and laugh occasionally, it was so rewarding. I also loved being able to care for Stella during the day and be home for my daughters by the time they returned home from school. Unfortunately, my caring for Stella became more and more physically draining and difficult for me. She needed breathing treatments, physical therapy twice a day, daily enemas, cool down baths when she developed high fevers, and injections of Valium to help combat occasional seizures.

Eventually, I reluctantly left my job with Stella and went to work three days a week for Dr. Parr, an ophthalmologist. I found it exciting to be his surgical nurse, assisting with his eye surgeries. It was during this time that my old enemy, depression, returned to stay for a while. Painful memories from my past were returning, and so were the vivid nightmares. The resulting insomnia made it very difficult to function at my job during the day. I began losing periods of time that I could not account for. I would find myself at the mall or the grocery store and have no idea how I got there. This also happened while I was driving. I would suddenly "come to" and find myself driving—to where I did not know.

Scarier still was that I also realized I was hearing voices inside of my head. At first I thought the voices were just my inner voice that everyone hears. I went to several therapists during this time and was given several different diagnoses, none of which explained what was happening to me. I would just start crying for no apparent reason. I would try and hide these seemingly involuntary emotions from Lorie and Christy, but as smart as they were, they no doubt knew that something was going on with mom.

Christy was in the sixth grade, and Lorie was in the ninth grade. I found this to be an extremely challenging time to parent my girls. Christy was angry all of the time, and I could do nothing for her that was helpful. Neither girl liked what I cooked for them. They told me they hated everything I served them, so I stopped cooking for them. I left them to fend for themselves.

I was still at the eye clinic, and I still loved it there. Even though my home life was incredibly stressful, after about a year with Dr. Parr, I began to work full-time. I was now assisting with all eye surgeries, including circulating for major eye surgeries. I was also the only minor surgery assistant. I would spend time assembling the surgery charts, cleaning the operating suite, sterilizing instruments, and injecting dye for fluorescence angiographies. I was also in charge of quality assurance.

As happy as I was at my job, I was miserable with myself. I just did not want to live anymore and attempted suicide by overdosing on my psychiatric medications. I ended up in the emergency room of another local hospital. From there I was admitted to a psychiatric hospital several miles from our house. I hated it there! One morning, early in my stay there, all of the patients, including me, were on the morning walk around the grounds. It was during this walk that I decided to leave. I walked home through the desert. My psychiatrist, Dr. Hanna, was called, and she sent the police to my home. By the time the police arrived, I had already been home and taken the car. Christy was home alone when the police arrived looking for me. Christy didn't know where I was and could only explain that I was not there. The police searched the house and grounds anyway but turned up empty handed.

I eventually returned home that day. Robert returned me to the hospital the next day, but this time to attend the day program. After Robert dropped me off and went to work, a nurse told me I would have to be readmitted all over again. Knowing what a long process this was, I wanted nothing to do with it and left the hospital a second time, walking home again. This time the police did not come. I was not readmitted to the hospital. Instead, Robert bought a safe and locked up all of my medications. Later, when one of my alters began to cut me with razor blades, he locked those up too. Because I could no longer distinguish between actual people talking to me and those voices I was hearing inside of my head, I qualified to receive disability insurance. This assistance eventually turned into long-term disability.

During this time in my life, I was being treated by psychologist, Dr. Barb Resse. She had suspected that I had multiple personality disorder, now called dissociative identity disorder[3] (DID). This disorder is usually formed in childhood as a result of horrific abuse. It causes the child's personality to shatter into many pieces without the child knowing. Each piece, known as an alter personality or fragment, holds the traumatic memory and protects the child from having to deal with the abuse. An alter personality can hold many memories; often a fragment just holds one.

She did not make that her official diagnosis, however. Instead she sent me to the Susan Forward Therapy Center in Los Angeles. My therapist there was Norma Vieton. After seeing Norma a few times, I began describing my nightmares to her. It was her determination that I was suffering from some form of sexual or ritual abuse that had occurred in my childhood.

In a therapy visit with Norma one day, I was talking with Norma when a small child's voice came out of my mouth. The child said her name was Naunie and that she was five years old. I was completely unaware of this phenomenon. One minute I was talking with Norma at the beginning of my session, and the next minute, or so it had seemed, I was at the end. When I came back into the conversation, I heard Norma talking with Robert. She was telling him that I had multiple personality disorder. She advised a five-year-old personality named Naunie had come out and talked with her.

I felt confused and scared but a little relieved all at the same time. At last there was some validation, some conformation to all of the mental hell I had been experiencing. As the weeks and months went by, Robert drove me the two and a half hours each way to my therapy appointments with Norma. I would see her every Saturday, where more and more personalities would begin to emerge.

Some personalities were very forthright; others emerged more shyly. Some of the earliest personalities we identified were Naunie, age five; Rosie, also age five; Joe, age eight; Suzie, age thirteen; and George, an adult male. There were many, many more personalities that would emerge, along with fragments of personalities who would usually just hold one memory. At one point, Norma and I had uncovered at least one hundred personalities and/or fragments.

Through therapy, Norma and I were able to determine that the sexual abuse started when I was three years old, with the rape from my father. It continued until I was sixteen, being raped by my father, brother, and many other men that my father shared me with.

Naunie's earliest memory took place at age three:

The floor was cold under my tiny feet as I ran around the house pushing my brother's truck around on the floor. I did not know where my mom and brothers were, but Dad was in the driveway working on a car. I was wearing a blue dress with little blue flowers on it. As I was playing in the bedroom, I heard the heavy wooded screen door slam shut. I was afraid, so I ran into the closet to hide. I heard my dad open the refrigerator to get another beer. Suddenly, he appeared at my doorway. I could hardly breathe because I was so afraid. I thought that if I took a deep breath, my father would hear me and find me hiding in the closet. I sat very, very quietly, hoping he would go away.

All of the sudden, the closet curtain was pulled back. I saw my father's angry face. He grabbed me by my arm, putting his beer down on the top of my dresser. "You can't hide from me!" he said in an angry tone of voice. He pulled me out of the closet and across the room. He tossed me onto the bed and pulled off my panties. Grabbing my left leg, he pulled me toward him. I tried to kick him and scoot away, but he held onto my leg so that I could not move.

I felt a stinging pain, and I cried, "No Daddy! No Daddy!" He did not stop. When he was finished, he left me laying there on my bed. He picked up his beer and went back outside.

This was my earliest memory to emerge. Now that I'm an adult, I know the abuse must have started when I was even younger than three. At three, I was already very afraid of my father.

Rosie held a memory of my brother, Larry, raping me when I was five years old:

It was cold and windy outside in the small, rural desert town where we lived. My brothers slept in the room attached to the garage called "the cabin." It was a small room that held two sets of twin bunk beds. The bunks were the kind used in the barracks at an army base. They were all metal with small mattresses on them. I begged my mother to let me sleep in the cabin with the big boys. Larry was sixteen, Pete was eight, and Mike was six years old at that time. I slept in the cabin on the floor in a sleeping bag, and I felt very grown up.

During the night, I got cold, so I climbed into bed with Larry. Larry had always protected me from my brother Mike. Even though Mike was only one year older than me, he would beat me up a lot. Larry's bed was warm, and I felt safe there. In the middle of the night, I awoke to feeling a searing pain between my legs. I cried out, "Stop! Stop!" The pain was excruciating. I could not breathe from his weight on top of me, his chest pressed tightly against my face as he raped me. Finally it was over. Blood poured onto the sheets on Larry's bed. I was not able to sleep from the severity of the pain. It felt like a sharp knife had been forced inside of me, slicing me open as it went in.

In the morning, Larry got up early to wash his sheets; he used the hose in the yard. I put my panties on and went inside. I never told anyone what had happened to me that night. I know I had blood on my underwear, but my mother never mentioned it.

By the time I was eight years old, my sexual abuse had been going on for many years. At that point it was becoming more frequent and more violent. Mom and I were folding towels at the kitchen table one day when I decided to pull together all of my bravery and strength and tell her what my father had been doing to me. I said, "Dad is doing bad things to me down there," pointing between my legs.

Without an ounce of hesitation, Mom said to me, "Better you than me!" She never once asked me what Dad was doing or showed any concern for my well being or my feelings. She only thought that it was better for him to sexually abuse me than her. This, I think, is very indicative of my mother being abused in her past. My mother had insinuated to me several times about her troubled childhood and how many things happened to her, but she'd never divulge just what those things were. From that day on, my mother always treated me like I was the "other woman."

I'm sure my mom had to have been overwhelmed most of the time. My father was a raging alcoholic and would beat my mother, brothers, and me. My mother left Dad three times, divorcing him each time, but was always forced to take him back. She had no other way to support her family financially.

Chapter 11

My Father

My Father

My father was born in Oklahoma. He was one of ten children in a very poor family. When the Great Depression came, and during the Dust Bowl, he and his family moved to the Modesto, California, area. My father's mother was half Cherokee Indian and was a devoutly religious woman; the family attended the Pentecostal church. They went to church almost daily. My father's mother was very strict and ruled the roost in her family. Dad grew to hate his mother and rebelled from all religion. As an adult, he claimed to be an atheist.

My father left school when he was just a sixth grader so he could go to work and help support his family. As a young man, Dad left home and became a hobo, riding the train rails across the country. When he returned to the Modesto and Fresno areas in California, he went to work in the fields and canneries.

He eventually married, but this marriage did not work out; my father was already an alcoholic, and so was his wife. Together they had three children: Jack, Janice, and Larry. When Dad left his wife to marry my mother, he brought his three children with him.

It was no secret that in his household, my father was a mean and angry man. He never said a kind word to his wife or children. By the time I was five years old, my youngest brother Sam came along. Sam made the seventh child in our blended and very hurting family.

When I was eight months old, our father moved us from northern California to Hansonville, California, a small, rural desert town. Dad took a job in the motor pool at the Air Force base. Although I know that he served in World War II, I don't know what his ending rank was nor how long he was in the service.

We lived in a very small two bedroom house. The only bathroom was situated so that in order to get to the bathroom, one would have to pass through my parent's bedroom. I was always so scared to go to the bathroom at night. I don't recall exactly what I was afraid of, but suspect it was that he would follow me in and rape me. It is highly likely that these fears may indeed have already been actualized, but on a conscious level, I had blocked the actual events out of my memory. All that remained was a very vivid and all-too-real fear.

I know now that my father was a pedophile. I believe he would, and likely did, molest any child he could get his hands on. My father told me one day that he had sex with my half-sister Janice, so why should I be any different. I never heard my father speak with nice language; it was always cuss words strung along in a sentence, like a beaded necklace. My father was also a prejudiced person. He had hateful names for everyone, but he especially hated black people. I know he owned a Klu Klux Clan hood and robe. He would wear it when a gang of men would gather at Black Canyon to molest the female children they had secretly brought there.

My father would beat us children with his belt. We were all very afraid of him. I remember that he drank beer constantly and harder liquor sometimes too. He smoked cigarettes so much that a constant blue haze hung around our house. My father beat up my mother and belittled her in front of us children.

I can honestly say that I hated my father and will never mourn his death. My life has always been a happier place to live without my father in it. At Christmas and Thanksgiving time, my dad would drink so much alcohol that he would frequently pass out on the bathroom floor. My brothers could go pee outside, but I could not or would not. I remember tip toeing into the small bathroom, being so scared that my dad would wake up. It was as if he were a large bear lying on the floor. This experience ruined any happiness that I might have felt on those holidays.

Chapter 12

My Siblings

My Siblings

In my family, I am not the only one to have suffered. It seems likely that my father was also physically abusing my brothers. They, too, became sexually active with me from the time that I was in kindergarten or first grade.

Although Pete stopped molesting me when I was in the second or third grade, Mike continued until I left home at age sixteen. When I think back about what Pete was doing to me, it seems less like molestation, and more like childhood sexual curiosity. Trying to make Mike stop forcing me to have sex with him was futile; if I didn't give it freely like Mike wanted, he would take it from me forcibly.

Mike was also cruel to me as I was growing up. When my breasts started developing, he would punch me as hard as he could in the chest. I have always suspected that part of the reason my alter named Joe exists is due to this abuse. Mike had a few girlfriends in high school and was abusive to them; he called them "slut" and "bitch." His treatment of women disgusted me. He obviously learned his lessons well from our dad.

Mike ended up marrying four to five times, but the marriages always ended with the same result. They never worked out. Mike was abusive to all of his wives. Again it was, "Monkey see, monkey do." Mike was also an alcoholic, but is sober now and has developed a relationship with God.

Pete was always quiet and sensitive. He pretty much kept to himself. Pete married a woman several years older than himself, who already had two children. They ended up having two more children together. Pete seems happy in his marriage, but we don't really talk. He does not seem to want to have anything to do with me. I think this is because he is afraid I will tell his wife about the sexual contact he had with me when we were young. I don't blame Pete, however; he was young and was probably abused just like me. He was likely just doing as he was told.

Sam is my youngest brother. He had a few children before he married at the age of forty-eight. Sam still lives in the area where we grew up. When we last spoke, he still owned the house we grew up in.

Larry, my half-brother, is eleven years older than me. I loved and trusted him very much until I was five years old and he raped me. He married in his teen years, having two children before he divorced. He, too, was abusive to his wife. Larry remarried, moved to Needles, California, and had at least one other child, a daughter. I do not have any contact with him and do not ever intend to.

Jack is my father's oldest son. I think Jack is about seventeen years older than me, although I am not sure because he left home when I was small. I was never abused by Jack. When he was younger, Jack stole a car and was sent to a boys home. He joined the military, where he became an adult. He married young and had a son. Sadly, just after their son was born, Jack's wife died during heart surgery. Jack eventually remarried, but it was to the daughter of one of my dad's best friends, who had also molested me.

Janice is my father's first daughter. She was sixteen when I was born and left home when I was around a year old, not finishing high school. My dad told me once that he molested Janice too, but she refuses to talk with me about this; I can only guess that it is a fact. Janice got married around age seventeen. She did her best to parent her three children; I am sure she found it difficult since she had also lacked a role model for parenting. Her husband drank way too much beer, but did work hard to support his children. It is sad that the legacy of dysfunction has been passed on to the next generation yet again.

I know that by marrying Robert and raising our daughters the way we did, we interrupted the cycle of abuse that was a part of the lives of me and my siblings. What a blessed gift to my brand new grand-daughter who joined our family this year! I feel so hopeful for her future.

Chapter 13

Intensive Therapy
Intensive Therapy

I turned forty years old in 1992 and would be in intensive therapy for the next several years. I felt out of control and suicidal much of the time. Lorie was away at college at this point, but I did talk with her every day. I missed her terribly. This time was especially hard for Christy. She had just started high school. Each day she was afraid she would come home from school and find her mother dead.

I was unable to function as a mother or a wife then. Over one hundred personalities would emerge over the following two years, with many frightening memories that would follow. My doctor at the time, Dr. Hanna, was prescribing antidepressants and anti-anxiety medications. Having insomnia, I could never sleep well, so I was always wandering all over the house through those wee hours. Without Dr. Hanna's assistance and expertise with my medications, I feel like I would have probably killed myself. She always knew what medication I needed at the time, and which ones I didn't. We both had an agreement that I did not want to be "overmedicated" to the point of feeling numb. She worked hard to keep me sane.

When Lorie came home from college in 1992, she wanted to marry her high school boyfriend. She found a job and attended school at the local junior college. She and her boyfriend lived in an apartment. Christy and I were not getting along. I took her to a therapist, but this did not work out well, as Christy refused to talk. She would sit in the therapist's office, staring at the floor, refusing to talk, so the sessions ended after a few attempts.

By 1994 I had been in a psychiatric hospital a few times. I had begun to develop an eating disorder. At times I would starve myself, and at other times I would stuff myself with junk food to soothe my emotions. I gained a lot of weight.

How Robert withstood all of this from me, I'll never understand. I do not have enough words to fully explain how unwavering Robert's support was toward me or how grateful I am to him for always being there when I needed him the most. Through all of this, Robert stuck it out with me. He read books on multiple personality disorder and how best to treat it. He also read a book on sexual healing after childhood sexual abuse. Robert would talk with my new alters as they would emerge and talk with them on the way to and from my therapy sessions in Los Angeles. I now had complete control over our sex life, as Robert no longer pressured me for sex. When I felt comfortable having sex, I could initiate it. This was so pivotal to my success in the therapy work I was doing at that time. It was also a major turning point in my marriage.

Around this same time, I was feeling pressure from

my therapist. It was a confusing period in my life. She believed, as did other therapists at that time, that only satanic cult abuse could have caused my personality to split. I disagree with this. I believe that any severe child abuse can cause the personality to split.

Through diligence and the strength that can come with being a survivor, I dared to look within to try and determine the "reality" of my memories. I needed to figure out which memories I had actually experienced and which ones were fiction. I knew for sure that while I *was* ritually abused by my father and his "good ole boy" pedophile friends around a bonfire at Black Canyon, I could not say for certain that there was any satanic cult activity going on. More likely, I believe it was just an out of the way place where this group of drunk monsters could get away with the abuse.

Since I could not be as certain as my therapist wanted me to be, I broke free from the hold I felt she had on me. To this day, I still struggle with a handful of memories of a more satanic nature. I am unsure whether these memories actually took place or were the result of therapeutic suggestion during these early counseling sessions. I will never know, and because I was not sure, I opted to leave them out of this memoir.

When I went back to work at the another eye surgery center, where I worked three days a week and cared for the surgical patients in pre-op. I joined a diet program and lost eighty pounds. Robert and I started bike riding, and I felt so much healthier. Since things were all going so well and I was feeling better than I had in a long time, I felt that I no longer needed therapy and tried to put all of that behind me.

I continued to work at the eye surgery center until December 1996, when I once again became very ill.

I was nauseous, dizzy, and had headaches all of the time, so I returned to Dr. Thompson. He ordered another CAT scan, and it was discovered that the hydrocephalus had returned due to the regrowth of the cyst in my brain. I went back into surgery where an AV shunt was inserted in my brain. I was only in the hospital for a few days. My recovery was uneventful. I was preparing to return to work toward the end of January 1997 when I once again developed terrible headaches. I was readmitted to the hospital, where my neurosurgeon ordered an MRI Scan. The scan found that I had something called slit ventricle syndrome. This is where my shunt was pumping out too much fluid, so my ventricles had collapsed. The old shunt was removed and replaced with one that opens at a higher pressure. I did not snap back this time and ended up being unable to go back to work.

By June of 1997, I started back with a marriage and family therapist named Janet whom I had seen on and off for several years. Although she had been giving me emotional support and would occasionally talk with some of my alters or deal with the incest memories, I would always leave feeling frustrated. All of my memories were still feeling very traumatic to me. I felt dead inside. While talking about my memories, I would feel all of the anger and sadness surrounding the trauma. I felt so empty. I found it hard to have meaningful relationships, and I would isolate from everyone. I tried hard to be loving with my husband and girls, but I could never quite get there. Something was missing. I could not feel a sense of joy or true happiness. Holidays, like Christmas, would come and go, but they would feel just like another day to survive.

That's what life was for me: just surviving from one day to the next.

In order to combat my depressing numbness, I made a decision to return to school. I took the drug and alcohol counseling program at the local junior college. It helped a lot to take my mind off of the DID and depression diagnosis I was entrenched in. This was not enough, however, so I also attended Chapman University to finish my BS degree in Health Sciences.

It was during this time when I was also needed to care for my elderly mother-in-law, who had just been diagnosed with Alzheimer's Disease. I would care for my mother-in-law during the day. We took long walks and would play board games to try and assist with her cognitive functioning. We would read the newspaper every day and watch the Oprah show in the afternoon. While Lorene napped, I would do my homework. We went on like this for a couple of years and had a wonderful time together, whether we were preparing lunch or talking about my daughters and parenting.

As part of my drug and alcohol program, I was required to do an internship two days a week. This took place at an inpatient alcohol and drug recovery program near home. I worked with the female patients there, doing intakes, counseling, and running groups. I learned a lot about addiction and how recovery takes place while I was there.

I graduated from Chapman University with a BS degree in health science by the time I was forty-seven years old. I also earned a certificate in mediation and anger management. By November of that same year, I went to work for Hospice. I worked three or four days a week, visiting patients in their homes and in convalescent centers. I continued in talk therapy with Janet, but it did not seem effective in dealing with my DID. When I found myself between therapists, Janet was always someone I could turn to. Sometimes I think I had to get tired enough of the familiar before I could make any headway with anyone else. For this reason, I feel Janet was an important part of my treatment. She helped me to deal with the day-to-day issues which were separate from my diagnosis. She helped me to cope with my life. When I was ready, I would always seem to find another therapist and start working on my deeper issues once again.

I had an interesting system set up with my alters as I worked in Hospice. George is the educated nurse, so he would give the physical care to the patients. He also got me from one appointment to the next in the car. Suzie did all of the psychiatric nursing, giving competent, emotional support to the patients, while Naunie and Joe stayed out of my work altogether. I was the overseer for all of the aspects of my job.

A typical day could look like this: George would get us to an appointment and do the physical nursing; Suzie would take over for the psychiatric nursing. When I left a given home, I would still be Suzie, but Suzie had a horrible sense of direction. I would have to stop the car and allow George to re-emerge so he could take control and find the next patient's house. The patients did not know that I was changing alters, they just knew me as Dauna.

I loved being a Hospice nurse, and I think I did my job well. The patients' love for me seemed to speak to how well of a job I must have been doing. I continued in this type of nursing for four and a half years. It was during this time with Hospice that I found a new therapist.

Dauna Cole

This symbol means
HELP. I made
This symbol as a
child and put it
on almost all of
my school papers.

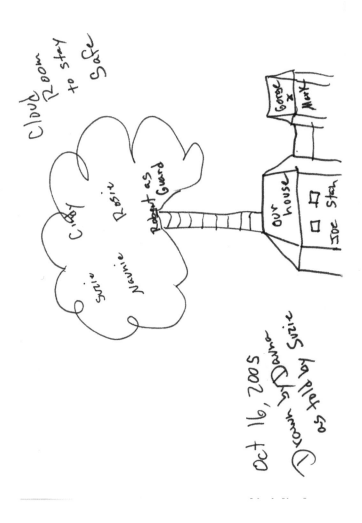

Cloud Room to stay Safe

Cindy

Suzie

Robin

Navnie

Robert as Guard

Our house

Joe Stach

Goroc x Mart

Oct 16, 2005

Suzie

ha plot so

Donna

Drawn by

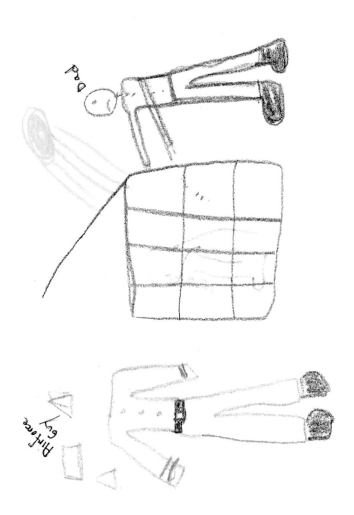

Every christmas my Dad
Would get drunk and pass
out on the bathroom
Floor. I Was afraid
to go to the Bathroom
all day. Sometimes I
had to urinate in
the yard. Memory
of cindy.
written by Dauna

12-16-04
Dauna

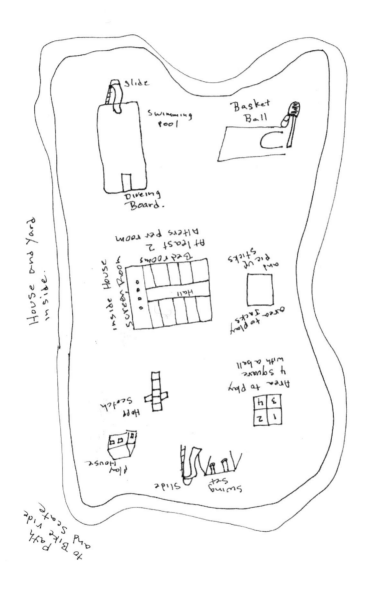

Dauna Cole

Chapter 14

Rosie's Memory

Rosie's Memory

While watching television one day, a policeman was talking about how he would go into chat rooms on the internet to find pedophiles. Robert told me not to watch that show, but of course, I did anyway. The chat room the policeman entered was a room where people talk about having sex with children and sometimes incest as well. One man on the internet talked about how sweet it is to have sex with your daughter.

That was all it took for an alter named Rosie to emerge with a memory from when I was two or three years old. My father had picked me up and sat me on his lap. His pants were unzipped, and he did not wear underwear. He pulled my little yellow dress over his hand, hiding what he was doing as he molested and raped me. I tried to squirm away, but he held me tight. My brothers were sitting on the couch right next to where I was; my mother was just a few steps away in the kitchen. I cried out, "No, no, no, daddy," and he let go of me. I ran to the kitchen and held on to my mom's leg. She pulled away from me, saying, "I'm busy with dinner now. Why don't you go play?" I went into my bedroom and lay down on my bed.

Chapter 15

Progress

In 2004, I realized I had been in and out of therapy for thirty years. I realized, too, that I would talk about the same things over and over again, remembering the heinous childhood abuse that I survived. The memories were just as fresh as if I was a young girl. I had spent thousands of dollars on talk therapy, and for what? Only to find myself in my fifties, still sad and angry. I thought that there must be a better treatment out there to help heal this pain.

I remembered something my psychiatrist had told me about a psychologist named Dr. Richards who was offering a new kind of therapy called EMDR[4] and Life Span Integration[5]. I decided to make an appointment with her, and from my first hour with Dr. Richards, I felt better! In session, she would put headphones on my head with quiet music transferring from one ear to the other. Dr. Richards also gave me small discs to hold in my hands. Each disc would vibrate for a few seconds, then the vibration would alternate from one disc to the other. This process was designed to help me transfer my traumatic memories from the feeling side of my brain to the intellectual side of the brain; the left versus the right side. The EMDR process would take the fear, anger, and pain away from each memory.

Around two a.m., I awoke with a startle. I was coconscious with a nonverbal infant. I could hardly breathe, and I had a nasty taste in my mouth. The infant was choking and making a grunting sound. I tried to speak to wake Robert up but found that I could not. I felt completely helpless and trapped inside this alter. I felt like something was being forced into my mouth. The infant was very frightened and shaking all over. I was crying uncontrollably.

I kicked Robert with my foot to wake him. He immediately knew just what to do. He held me and my infant self in his arms and stroked our forehead. He talked softly to us and told us that everything would be fine and that it was just a bad memory. He continued saying that the bad men were all gone now; they were all dead and would never hurt us again. He said, "I'm your good daddy, and I will protect you."

As quickly as this alter came, she disappeared into the darkness of my mind. I was left feeling shaken and scared. I could still taste the nasty, salty taste in my mouth. I found it difficult to breathe. I was able to tell Robert what had just happened to me and how it felt to be trapped in this infant's body. It was the most frightening, helpless feeling I have ever had.

We turned on the light and got out of bed. I sat in the recliner in the living room with a soft blanket over me. Robert brought me a glass of soda to drink. I sipped it slowly and eventually the taste began to disappear. Eventually, I stopped shaking and was able to go back to sleep.

After I would talk about an upsetting memory like the one above, Dr. Richards would take the alter who was holding that particular memory to a safe place. After that, she would bring the alter forward in time, one year at a time, by having me remember something else that may have happened that year. For example, I loved to play with the big wooden trucks in kindergarten. I loved to play tetherball in the third grade. We would do this technique until I was my current age. Then Dr. Richards would ask my alter if she/he wanted to come inside me to a safe place where there were, by that time, other children to play with. If the alter agreed, the therapist would ask me to close my eyes and feel the alter merging into my chest. Each time I would do this process, I would feel a peaceful warmth in my chest and a deep sense of relaxation. It was the first time that I felt I was getting the help I needed.

In one session, I experienced, or I should say, I re-experienced my birth. With my therapist's guidance, I closed my eyes and imagined I was back inside my mother's womb. My mother was in labor, and I felt the sensation of pressure surrounding my whole body. Then I began to feel pressure around my head and chest as I passed through the birth canal. I thought it would feel like I was suffocating, but thankfully, it didn't.

The umbilical cord was wrapped around my neck twice when I was born, and I was blue. In my rebirthing session, I had the sensation that I was hanging upside down and could feel the snaps to the soles of my feet when the doctor was trying to get me to breathe. Suddenly, I felt a sharp pain in my lungs when I took my very first breath. I could hear myself crying.

Following my rebirth, Dr. Richards led me forward in time through the first three months of life. There was nothing significant until we reached six months of age. I recalled suddenly feeling a sharp pain in my vagina, and I started to really cry in pain. Both Dr. Richards and I felt that this was my father or someone inserting his finger into my vagina. It was very likely that this was when the first sexual abuse began.

I was too upset to continue, so Dr. Richards quickly moved me and my six-month-old self through to integration. After integrating my infant self, I felt calmer. That session left me with a profound sense of sadness. What kind of man would do such a thing? I felt the loss of my infancy, like a part of me had died inside. In my past work with therapists, I had found it difficult to experience emotions, good or bad, and that rebirthing exercise was the first time I really connected to my feelings and to what had happened to me in my life. I now realized that the abuse did not happen to my alters, it happened to me! It was from this understanding that I could begin integration work, and the alters who were ready could finally begin to integrate.

Integration wasn't a quick process by any means, but I was on my way to becoming my authentic self. Integration represented major progress in working through my DID. The sadness began to lift from me, bit by bit. I could finally begin to think about, talk about, and write about the memories without feeling the pain and sadness. I want to add that Life Span Integration therapy isn't for everyone, nor is it the be all and end all of therapy modalities for someone with DID. This was a good option for me at the time because I wasn't responding to anything else. I believe this form of therapy helped me to let go of the constant fear and pain I lived with and become a person that could relax and begin to enjoy life.

When I was in therapy with Dr. Richards, it was so traumatic uncovering so many frightened little children inside of me. I needed a place where they could go to feel safe. With the help of Suzie and Naunie, we created a "cloud room" inside of me. This room is in the sky and is surrounded by clouds. There is a ladder going up to it that my alters can pull up after themselves so no one can follow them. The cloud room is soft and quiet. George or Joe stays below the cloud room to keep the bad men from coming up to bother the alters there. I find myself, even today, going into the cloud room when I am feeling stressed or afraid. It is a safe place for me.

My "inside house" is another place I have created for my alters. While in therapy, I discovered that I had all of these children inside of me, but they had nothing to do. They were constantly clamoring for my attention. I heard their voices inside of my head all of the time; I liken it to being in the middle of a kindergarten classroom. I figured out that if I gave them a place to play and things to do, they stayed happy and quiet. The "inside house" has many bedrooms. It has a screening room, where the alters can watch me living my life and keep track of what is going on with me. There is also a play area.

At one point in therapy, Dr. Richards asked me to go "inside" and play with the children one by one. I think she thought it would be beneficial to acknowledge them individually. This was actually more harmful than helpful. It caused them to talk louder and vie for my attention even more when I wasn't there. After I stopped trying this, it slowly got quieter again.

Chapter 16

More Pain and Anguish

By May of 2004, while still working for Hospice, I began to feel the effects of all of the deaths I had experienced as a hospice nurse. Everywhere I drove my car, I would think about a particular patient I had treated who had lived and died there. I'd find myself crying in between stops. It almost felt like I was being haunted by my deceased clients; it was definitely time for a change.

I had always wanted to be involved in obstetric nursing and thought it would be so rewarding to help bring new little lives into the world, saying hello to my patients rather than always saying good-bye as in hospice nursing. In order to make this happen, I trained at the local hospital as a labor and delivery trainee. In class, I learned how to read the monitors and strips, as well as learn about babies' heart rates during labor, monitoring vital signs, and newborn assessments. I loved most everything about this job, especially giving the newborns their first bath. They especially loved getting their head/hair washed. They would relax and stretch. The babies were adorable, and it was so rewarding to work with healthy, strong women.

After learning about labor and delivery, I learned about Cesarean sections. Little did I know that this training would be my undoing. Almost right away, I found this to be very frustrating because I never felt I had enough time to get everything done in such a short period of time.

There was a lot of bending, squatting, pushing, and pulling, and my back started hurting after the first couple of days. By the end of that summer, I could no longer stand the pain. It got to the point one day where even trying to get dressed in my work scrubs caused immense pain. I went right to the employee health station at the hospital, and they sent me to the emergency room. I explained to a doctor about the intense low back and shoulder pains and pain at the base of my neck. I was given a pain shot, anti-inflammatory medication, muscle relaxants, and a general medication for pain, and I was sent home for the weekend.

On Monday, I went to see an orthopedist named Dr. Leeman. It felt like he had not taken into account that I'd been on medication all weekend. He only said, "You are fine. Go back to work." I was happy to be going back to work, however, and looked forward to the following day when I would be returning to my shift. The next day was an extremely long day even under ordinary circumstances; it was a thirteen-hour day with only a ten minute break. Because I was still on medications, I did not immediately feel the pain that my work was causing me. I was still assisting with Cesarean sections and not even realizing that I was reinjuring my back. By the end of my shift, I was in so much pain that I could barely walk to my car. Driving home was very painful. Even after a few days off, my condition did not improve. Once again, I could not even get dressed into my scrubs, so my nursing supervisor sent me home and to urgent care. That doctor put me back on the same medications that Dr. Leeman had taken me off of. I would spend my days with ice packs and in tears. I went to see a new orthopedist eventually. He ordered an MRI of my lumbar spine. The workman's compensation company that represented my place of employment denied the request. After several denials, I went to employee health to talk with the nurse there. She was cold and unfeeling, refusing to help me. I hired a lawyer and got my MRI approved right away.

That was in 2004 and just before I began seeing Dr. Richards. After spending much time and money on several types of treatments like physical therapy, acupuncture, chiropractic, and steroid injections, I still ended up needing surgery. In June of 2006, I had a Laminectomy[6] and fusion of my L-4 and 5 vertebrae. At this writing, it is 2008, and although I feel better overall, I still have pain in my lumbar and cervical spine and cannot lift over fifteen pounds. I find house work daunting, and yard work is out of the question. I will never again be able to be a primary care nurse.

With all of the changes I was enduring—both emotionally and physically—it was no surprise that I began to feel suicidal again. I tried acupuncture for the depression, but it brought back more childhood memories. I began to remember my experiences with a doctor my mother would take me to when I was about five years old. As a little girl, I suffered from constant earaches and vaginal infections. I would be treated by Dr. Muster in Hansonville, California.

When I went to see Dr. Muster, there were times that he would take out a black box with a crank on top. This box had a wire coming out of the side of it, and at the other end of the wire was a needle-like probe. The doctor would turn the crank handle around and around and shock my hands and feet with the needle-like tip. He did this in order to force me to have oral sex with him. Sometimes he would be satisfied if I just touched his penis. Dr. Muster was also a member of the pedophile group my dad hung out with.

He was a big man, and I was always very afraid of him. I would cry whenever I had to see him. I remember his office was a room that was connected to his house, and there were never any nurses to help him in his office. My mother would never come in to the exam room with me. I vividly remember the black table I had to sit on when I was getting shocked. I could not handle these visits, so Naunie would come out and endure them for me. It was Naunie that would cry and scream and tell Doctor Muster, "No." The doctor would never stop; he would just shock me more, so Naunie eventually stopped reacting to the shocks and did as she was told, just like a little robot. After I started seeing Dr. Richards and shared the memory of Dr. Muster with her, Naunie and I were helped with the bad memories by changing the memory to where my mom got the shocks instead of me.

Because of Dr. Muster's shock treatment, the acupuncture episode that was meant to alleviate my back pain caused me to be reactive, like a flashback. I became withdrawn and suicidal later that afternoon while Robert was sleeping. Naunie took a razor blade and began to cut my left wrist, vertical to my arm where the artery was. When Robert walked out to the living room and saw what Naunie and I were doing, he said, "I do not like what I am seeing," and went back to bed. In retrospect, I think he was probably so sleepy that he did not even realize what was going on. Since he didn't try and stop me, we thought it meant he was saying it was okay for us to commit suicide. I saw Robert had left his keys on the dresser. This was the same key ring that held the keys to the safe where my medications were kept. We picked up the keys quietly and went to the office where the safe and my medications were locked up. We took a large bottle of Darvocet and a full bottle of Ambien and hid them; then we replaced the keys back on the dresser. After Robert went to work for the night, Naunie and I took three large handfuls of Darvocet and the full bottle of Ambien. We crawled into bed and fell into a dangerously deep sleep.

When Robert came home from work that morning, he was unable to wake me. He saw the empty bottle of Ambien but not the bottle of Darvocet. He thought I would sleep it off and was not alarmed enough to call 911. By noon, Lorie had called. When she found out I was still asleep and had taken the medication that Robert had thought I had taken, she became alarmed and called 911. The emergency squad arrived and rushed me to the hospital. The police also came and were very upset with Robert. They told him to never leave a suicidal person alone again, to always call 911 in the case of an overdose, no matter how mild he suspected it to be.

I remained in the emergency room in a coma for many hours. When I woke, I was angry that I was still alive and angry with Lorie for calling 911. Of course I'm glad now and know without reservation that Lorie did the right thing. I remained in the emergency room for five more hours and then was discharged to the psychiatric unit.

I remember being put in a hard bed, which made my sore back hurt intolerably. I was not allowed to have any pain medication. I was also not given a call light to ask for help when I needed it. I was angry and sad. I had talks with a social worker and psychiatrist. In the meantime, Robert had come with my clothes in a plastic bag. The plastic bag remained on the floor next to my bed for the rest of my stay, and if I had been coherent enough to try to kill myself again, I would have used that bag.

After being there for a few days, George, my male alter, took over for the sad, angry, and suicidal alter. George went to the psychiatrist and asked to be sent home. The psychiatrist, who apparently did not believe the DID diagnosis, was so surprised in the change in me. He agreed to send me home if I made an appointment with my therapist and a psychiatrist for the next day. After I did this, Robert came to take me home. I apologized to Lorie for being so angry with her, but I am still upset with myself for being angry with her when she was only trying to save my life.

Chapter 17

Robert's Story

The following entry was written by my husband, Robert in his own words. This is his take on life with a wife who lives with DID.

How I met Dauna. I was a junior at Loma Linda University in La Sierra, California, and had just transferred after graduating from a junior college. I met Dauna in my physiology class. Dauna bought herself a ten speed bike, so we started going for bike rides together. I had always been a very introverted person and found it really hard to talk with girls. Having dated one girl in my junior college, Dauna was only the second girl I'd ever dated. The nice thing with Dauna was that we were just friends who went on bike rides together.

I dropped out of school by the second semester because of dental problems I was having. Dauna, however, was afraid that I left school because she had told me about having her father's baby. At the time she told me about the baby, I told her that I still liked her and her past was not a problem for me.

The next school year, I attended another campus of the university. Dauna found me there and gave me a call. We started seeing each other again. I loved Dauna. Even though she had a bad childhood, she was a hard worker, very caring, truthful, and very mature. When Dauna began to have financial and psychological problems at school, she dropped out and began working at the hospital. We got married on June 16, 1972, after knowing one another for two years.

I have never been much of a talker, but after Dauna was diagnosed with her multiple personality disorder, I not only had to learn to talk to her scared kids (alters), I had to do this talking during the hours of two to four a.m. Before her actual diagnosis, there had been times during the night when Dauna would talk about her childhood but not remember what she had said in the morning. There were other times where she would not remember the same incidences we had each experienced the same way that I remembered them happening.

I know that a therapist needs to keep the client-therapist relationship confidential, yet I didn't know how to help her until I was able to have some information from Dauna's therapist. The therapist that diagnosed Dauna's DID did not want to talk with me as her husband. She did not want to tell me how to deal with the alter personalities when they would come out. This therapist did not want me to tell her things that happened with Dauna since the last time she had seen my wife.

The problem with DID is the secrets that are kept.

In a case where it affects a whole family, I feel that the whole family needs to be involved. The patient has secrets that have been kept from her by her alters. It is impossible for those secrets to come out only during one or two hours that the patient and therapist meet for a session. Sometimes Dauna did not know much about a therapy session because an alter was present for most of the session, and Dauna is not present mentally when an alter is out. The secrets of abuse kept by alters help to protect the core person from overwhelming feelings and memories.

I know that I am not a therapist, and over the years I have tried not to be the therapist, but as the husband of a woman with DID, I have had to deal with alters anytime, day or night. I feel that I am here to bring the alters into the present, letting them know that things have changed so they know they will never be abused again.

As I have mentioned, most of my encounters have been between the hours of two and four a.m. I'll be sleeping, and all of the sudden I feel the whole bed shaking, and the person in bed with me is crying and shaking with overwhelming fear and pain. I try to get a name and age and even a partial memory of what is happening. Some alters are male, but most have been female; most are younger than sixteen years old, with a few that are infants that cannot talk.

On occasion, a few adult male alters have appeared who want to hurt Dauna. We think of these alters as "internal enforcers." It seems their goal is to perpetuate the abuse. These internal enforcers have been real problems because they want to cut Dauna's body with knives or razor blades, take an overdose of pills, or even get a gun and shoot at the host's body. I've found it very hard to deal with things myself at times, but after Dauna wakes up, I can let her know a name, age, and partial memory so she can then get in touch with the help of her therapist.

It has been strange being with some alters. For example, I have gone into a Disney-animated movie with my wife and come out of the theater with a five-year-old girl talking about how much she liked to movie. I'd feel a little embarrassed walking with a forty-year-old woman who was talking in a very young, childish five-year-old girl's voice.

It has also been very interesting being with a young teenage boy alter. One time my wife and I went out on a windy day to fly a kite. Joe, the teenaged boy, came out after getting the kite up into the air. We talked about riding bikes and doing other things that boys like to do. After about thirty minutes, we brought the kite down and went home. Joe sat down in a recliner chair and wanted some ice cream. All Dauna remembered was getting the kite aloft one minute, and the next thing she knew, she was sitting in the recliner eating ice cream.

None of the male alters liked being in a female's body. Many times I have been out hiking with Joe when he wanted to stop and pee on a bush. I'd have to remind him that he has female plumbing!

It has been a very interesting thirty-five years (at this writing) being married to Dauna. Both of us have grown a lot and love each other more each day.

Chapter 18

Intimacy

It would be natural to wonder how someone with my history of abuse could handle the whole issue of sex and lovemaking. I have worked very hard to get to the level of acceptance and comfort I am today. Yes, there can even be enjoyment where making love is concerned. Before I delve further, I want to stress that this is very much a process that unfolded for me in my life.

As a child, every time I was raped and molested by my father and his friends, my life was threatened. From day to day, I did not know if I would live to be an adult. This made a connection for me between sex and death. I also did not know that sex was something you did with a boyfriend, lover, partner, or husband. Sex was frightening, painful, and something your dad forced you to do. When I got older and understood sex more, I feared that if I ever got to be an adult, I could never be sexual with anyone.

In adolescence, when I became friends with Dan, it never occurred to me to have sex with him. I never saw him that way. I loved Dan very much, especially after he offered to marry me and raise the baby as his own. He was a kind and intelligent person, but he was my friend. I haven't seen him since I was sixteen but will always be grateful to him for his gentleness and compassion. He was a true friend.

After I started dating Robert, I was concerned about sex. We remained friends a long time before sex was even in the picture. When we finally did have sex, I was relaxed because I was not expecting to have sex; it just happened secondarily—sort of accidentally. Also, I had known Robert for some time by then, and I already trusted him not to hurt me. Our trust led to relaxation. Gratefully, this caused my first experience with him to be one that felt wonderful. We gradually became physically closer after this, and sex happened on purpose, with my consent, for the first time in my life! It was no longer sex, but love-making.

After I was married and eventually had to take antidepressant medication, our lovemaking was more problematic for me. It became just sex again, and I began to dread it once more. I started to feel like a robot. When having sex with Robert, I would get close to climaxing, and suddenly I'd begin to shake and cry and feel totally out of control. It was frightening for both of us, and we eventually had less and less sex.

Once I was diagnosed with DID, I began taking antipsychotic medication, and my sex drive disappeared completely. We stopped trying to have sex. Robert read a book called *The Sexual Healing Journey: A Guide for Survivors of Sexual Trauma*[7]. This book talked about how to give me more control over sex and had many other good suggestions as well. I could decide when and if we made love. It was the best advice we have ever been given. Over time, I found myself beginning to relax about sex. No longer did I have to worry about Robert wanting to have sex with me in the middle of the night. Whenever I wanted to have sex with Robert, I would initiate it. Sometimes, I just wanted to be held close, and Robert was fine with that too.

Our sex life began to turn around. I began to want to make love to Robert and just feel close to him. Eventually, I was able to stop taking the antipsychotic medication when I began the Life Span Integration therapy. Thankfully, I once again began to crave having sex with Robert. At last I can say that it is about intimacy and lovemaking once again.

Chapter 19

Living with DID

Throughout my life, I have learned a lot about discrimination, mostly from firsthand experience. My first experience with it was when I found out I was pregnant. Although I hope our society is kinder today about this social situation, back then it was awful. As soon as the news got around my high school, students and teachers were treating me like an outcast. I was called a slut. Just before my baby was born, I had moved to a high school for unwed mothers. The teacher in that school was very religious. She looked down on her pregnant students, never missing a chance to tell us all how bad we were and how we had sinned against God. Instead of this teacher using her religion positively, she only showed us discrimination and judgment. Things were made so much harder for us than they had to be. When I went to the hospital to give birth, the nurses there treated me so badly; I was looked down on. They made me feel like I was garbage.

Over and over today, I feel discriminated against because of my psychiatric diagnosis. My insurance company will not cover it the same as a medical diagnosis. It feels so hypocritical to me when you consider that if I had a chronic medical condition like diabetes, my insurance would have no questions about paying for my care. Because I have a psychiatric condition, my insurance limits the amount of care I can get. It requires my therapist to fill out long forms to justify my continued care. The kind of discrimination that hurts the most, however, is when it comes from folks I thought were friends. They cannot handle that I have a psychological problem. They ask insensitive things: "Why are you still in therapy?" "Can't you just get over the past abuse and move on with your life?" "What's wrong with you anyway?" They show a lack of education, understanding, and compassion. Mostly, it seems they are afraid of my psychiatric diagnosis. Isn't this what is at the bottom of most discrimination anyway?

A psychiatric diagnosis does not make me stupid. When I had to go into a social security office, the clerks talked to me like I was a three-year-old. My IQ is higher than most, which is consistent with people who share this diagnosis. Social Security made my husband my payee and will now only talk with him. I guess this is customary for people who have mental health diagnoses. I'm not mentally retarded. I can handle my own affairs if allowed to do so.

Isn't it about time that we change the way we see mental illness? As a society, we need to reeducate ourselves. Just as we do not discriminate against people with inherited conditions or cancer, for example, we cannot place blame on the mentally ill for being sick. We have an extra burden in our lives to deal with, but otherwise we feel joy, depression, sadness, and pain just like everyone else. Ask questions before judging. Take time to understand the person. It is surprising how far an attitude of support will take someone with mental illness. I did not choose to be abused as a child, and the abuse was what caused the mental illness. Believe me, this was not a life I chose for myself.

As I mentioned earlier in this book, multiple personality disorder and dissociative identity disorder are one and the same. DID is the updated terminology because it is more inclusive of the different ranges of diagnosed dissociations. DID develops at a young age, typically five and under, and is usually due to severe sexual, physical, and ritualized abuse. There can also be a Satanic Ritual Abuse (SRA) component.

The disorder comes about when the young person cannot deal with the extreme fear and pain (often torture) they are faced with. They create another personality to be able to handle the abuse. This is survival at its best because it allows the main "core" personality to stay intact and live. As the abuse continues, more personalities or alters can be created to handle what the child is unable to. The core personality is unaware of the painful memories that are now being held by the alters. This is how a survivor with such a history can carry on undiagnosed for many years. This is also why DID is so hard to diagnose; the core personality does not remember most of their childhood since each alter holds a piece of their childhood memories.

As the alters begin to emerge from deep inside, the core personality begins to learn about the abuse via memories introducing themselves outright or in nightmares. That is how it began for me. I had horrible nightmares for about five years before I started to understand that my bad dreams were really memories of my abuse coming to the surface. Another way survivors start to remember is by having certain smells, sounds, or physical sensations/touches trigger an actual abuse memory. When I was a pregnant teenager, I thought the abuse had started when I was about twelve years old. As time went on, the alters started coming to my conscious mind. Slowly, and through much therapy, I began to have memories of the abuse starting before I was two years old.

Thinking back to my childhood, it seems like there were so many clues about my abuse to the people around me. Almost daily, I would fall asleep in class. My homework was seldomly done. I had trouble making eye contact with teachers or adults at school and was afraid to speak up in class. I isolated myself from classmates and feared making friends because I did not want them to find out what was going on at home. I also tried to spend as much time as I could at school so I would not have to go home; I volunteered to wash blackboards, would clean classrooms, and offered to help my teachers.

Another strange behavior was that I was constantly trying to break my arm. I remember slamming it against the tetherball pole and trying to break it on my desk. I am not sure whether this was to bring attention to my abuse, or to punish myself for being such a "bad person." I started getting migraine headaches in the third grade; they were probably brought on by the stress I was under. My elementary school discipline record was also very long. I was always acting out in class and getting sent outside to sit by the water fountain. Lastly, I had a little symbol that I wrote as a doodle on my classwork, or on my desk. The symbol contained the letters h-e-l-p, but it was not obvious. Strangely enough, I even found this symbol in my wedding album, so I continued writing it for a lot of years.

The following are some signs you may recognize in yourself, a loved one, or a patient:

- Very few, if any childhood memories.

- There may be voices inside of your head; they could be male, female, a child's voice, or all three.

- People tell you they saw you, talked with you, or even did something with you, and you have no memory of it.

- The gas tank in the car may be surprisingly empty or full, with the odometer numbers increasing, and you don't remember driving anywhere.

- You may find a different style of clothing in the closet than you are used to wearing and can't explain how those clothes got there.

- There are cigarettes in your purse, and you don't smoke.

- You may wake up in a stranger's bed, with no memory of how or why you are there.

- You may get lost easily, even not remembering how to find your way home. You may also lose your car in parking lots.

I experienced many of these signs when my alters started surfacing. I would "come to" from being in another alters' personality and not know where I was, how I got there, or how to get home from there. I also heard conversations in my head a lot; some alters have a comment about everything I do. I would look at a menu in a restaurant, and each alter would want something different to eat. If I was out buying donuts, I would have to get two or three different kinds to satisfy everyone. Gratefully, this doesn't happen anymore, but when it did, I gained so much weight. My alters would even eat food without me knowing it. My child alters liked to get up in the middle of the night and eat. Several times, an entire carton of ice cream would be gone from the freezer, and I had no memory of eating it at all. I was lucky that my two main alters, George and Suzie, were similar to me—my likes and dislikes—so when either of them would switch, it would not be noticeable by most people.

Each of my alters has a different voice. They also have their own mannerisms. For example, George has a deeper voice and a flat affect. He is unemotional and very businesslike. Suzie laughs a lot and tends to be more emotional; she will even cry at some commercials. Naunie talks like a five-year-old. Joe uses a lot of slang words and is more animated.

My alters come forward when they want to say or do something. This used to be troublesome because they would take over my body completely. I would be unaware of what was happening and would lose time. I have since learned to be co-conscious with most of them. That means the alter can come out, but I am still here and know what is going on. I had very little control over the switching between alters at first. Over time, I have learned to control it better. It still causes a few issues, however. Whenever I go to a child's movie, Naunie always comes out, and I miss the movie. I went to a restaurant one day and George came out and ordered ribs. Naunie ended up coming out when the ribs were served and did not know how to eat them. She was also afraid of the knife that came on the plate. Robert had to come to the rescue to cut my ribs apart and show Naunie how to eat them. One consistent sign that appears when I am going to switch alters is that I start yawning excessively. I also used to have headaches after I switched, but luckily this has subsided.

At one point in my life, I had an alter named Jackie who loved sex. She would tackle my husband and want to have sex with him without me knowing. Imagine how strange, confusing, and possibly troubling it was to have suddenly have switched back to my core personality in the middle of having sex. I also used to have a teenaged alter who loved to shop. She would buy clothes that I would find in my closet and never wear; this was a big money drain on our family.

Sometimes a personality can speak another language or play a musical instrument without the core personality being aware of it. I had an alter who could play the piano, while I could not. There were also times when an alter would come out and attend one of our daughters' school functions or meetings without me knowing. A few times, an alter volunteered to do something at the school and I would find out later I had dropped the ball and not done it. There were lots of parents and teachers upset with me.

I have two kinds of alters. The first is what I call a full, or complete, personality. In my case, these personalities are an exaggeration of one trait in my personality. These personalities can function on their own without me being in control. They can each take complete control of my body. These complete personalities cause me to lose time. They also serve a function. George is my intellect. He loves to go to school and is my "working" personality. Suzie is my emotional side and cries easily. She also loves to shop and hang out with my daughters. She also loves talking on the phone. Joe is my youthful, active side. He loves to hike and bike and enjoys camping. He always wants to come out when we are around a teenage boy. Naunie is my innocence. She is sweet, loves going to the movies, and loves cats.

The second kind of personality is what I call a fragment. These alters come to me with a name, age, sex, and usually carry one memory. The fragment of a personality will usually disappear after talking about her/his memory. These fragments cannot take control of my body. If they do not disappear on their own, I can integrate them myself.

At one point in my therapy, my therapist and I decided to try and integrate the complete personalities. They did not disappear, and they did not bond or join with my personality. It was like they were inside of me, sealed in a bubble separate from each other. I could no longer call on them for help in my daily life. Though I no longer lost time, I felt lost without them; I had a grief reaction to losing them. Thankfully, I was able to undo the integration, and now I have all of myself back.

I remember one day a long time ago when I had to have my vision checked. The optometrist checked my vision and wrote it down. During the exam, I ended up switching to George, who had completely different vision. I am not sure how this happened, or even how it was physiologically possible, but it did happen. When the doctor went to complete the exam, my vision had totally changed. My optometrist could not figure out what had just happened. He was concerned and wanted me to see a neurologist. I did not tell him about my DID diagnosis. I'm sure he is still wondering what happened.

When my daughters were young, an alter was assigned to each of them; they were Christy and Lorie's other mothers, Fran and Margaret, respectively. They were full personalities and could function independently from me. By the time I was aware of these alters, the girls were pretty much grown. Fran and Margaret loved to bake cakes and always gave my daughters individual attention. I don't believe my daughters even knew about their "other mothers" until they had almost completely disappeared when the girls were older. They never called them by name. Fran, Margaret, and George were not formed because of the abuse; they each had a function. George was formed when I was under stress to do well at the university. He eventually became my working personality. At Christmas, my child alters would sing Christmas carols. I would hear them inside of my head constantly. Naunie loved to sing "Frosty the Snowman" and would sing it over and over and over. From Thanksgiving until New Year's Day, I thought I was going to lose my mind completely.

Not all alters were good to me. When I was first diagnosed with DID, I had an alter whose sole job was to abuse the core personality, my body. The alter's name was Jack. He felt I had evil in my blood. With knives and razor blades, he would cut me in hopes of bleeding the evil out of me.

As a child, I was always sad at Christmas. Later, as

my daughters were growing up, I did my best to make Christmas a happy, fun time for them, yet I would find the holidays hard to take because of my past memories. When I became aware of the alters, each one would come out to Robert and request a gift. He had to shop for all of them. Each alter would come out and open his or her gift. And of course, Naunie would sing "Frosty the Snowman."

When I started to integrate my alters through Life Span Integration therapy, I became aware of all of my alters' memories. I also stopped losing time. I finally feel like a whole person and can now remember my whole life, past and present. Last Christmas was the best I ever had. For the first time, no one was singing in my head. There were no alters to buy gifts for. In fact, for the first time in so long, Robert and I bought a Christmas gift for each other. I felt so relaxed and free. My life right now is happy. I am finally free to enjoy every moment with Robert.

I can now integrate my fragments on my own without a therapist. The fragments usually show up around three a.m. They let Robert know they are there and usually give him their names, ages, sex, and a little about their memory of abuse. Robert reassures them and lets them know that all the bad men are gone now and they are safe. The following day, after Robert tells me about the alter, I take this information to talk with them myself. I will close my eyes and call the alter to come speak with me inside of my mind. I reassure them that they are safe now and thank them for protecting me when I was young and being abused. I ask the alter if he/she wants to enter my "inside house" and be with all of my other alters. If they agree, I tell them to look for the light inside (the light is where my heart is) and call for Suzie and Naunie. Suzie and Naunie act as the welcoming committee and help new alters get settled inside. After the alter integrates, I feel a warmth inside my chest.

Today, when a new alter with a new memory emerges, I feel a little bit sad that I am not finished with the process. I was molested and raped by so many men for so long that the process may never end. I have to learn to accept that fact. I don't like it, but I do accept it. Every year, I can see more growth in myself. I get to choose how I want to live, and I realize that my life is my present. I hope you do not get discouraged by my story and think it will take thirty years of counseling to get well. Things have improved in psychology. I was misdiagnosed for over twenty years before someone got it right. Treatment modalities have improved as well.

Recently, I found myself becoming more tired and worn down; I just felt like sleeping all of the time. I couldn't keep my house clean and did not even have the energy to work on hobbies I love. I also seemed to cry a lot. Having struggled with depression my entire life, I just thought it was that, and sought treatment. I started seeing a psychologist, but after several months it did not seem to be helping. I know I have had a high stress level my entire life, but thought that once I moved to beautiful Washington state, my stress would be relieved.

Looking for answers, I went to see a hormone doctor who ordered a twenty-four hour urine test. The test showed that I have been producing large amounts of cortisol. The cortisol was a byproduct of the stress cycle I had gotten myself into. It seems that a hormone imbalance was to blame for my symptoms.

My adrenal glands were exhausted from reacting to all of the cortisol in my system. I have started taking vitamin supplements and herbal medications and am finally feeling great. My energy is back. Over the years I have become so accustomed to thinking everything is always psychologically based, but this opened my eyes to the fact that something can be as simple as a hormone imbalance.

Chapter 20

Thoughts from my Daughters

Thoughts from my Daughters

When I started writing my memoirs, I began wondering how my daughters were impacted by my DID. I asked them to share their experiences. Below are their stories.

Lorie:

From an early age, I was aware my mother had grown up in a difficult family. I knew I would *never* meet my grandfather. I knew he was a monster. I don't recall my mother ever explaining in detail what he had done to her, but I knew there was sexual abuse. I also knew he had gotten her pregnant, and with that she had gained her freedom. It made me sick to think about my grandfather. In my early twenties, when I learned he was sick and dying in a hospital in Arizona, I dreamed of going to visit and "pulling the plug." I never went.

My grandmother, however, was a part of my life. I also met most of my uncles. They came to visit, and we also went to see them several times in the house my mother grew up in. The house was a tiny shack in the middle of nowhere. It was so close to the railroad tracks that it would rattle when the trains went by. As an adult now looking back, I have a hard time believing my mother would even step foot in that house again. Though my grandmother and I were never close, I was glad for the time we spent together. I have fond memories of her. It means a lot to me that my mother set the problems with her mother aside and gave me the opportunity to know her.

When I was growing up, I knew that my family was different than most. I had two parents who loved me. I had a mother who would ask me what I wanted to be for Halloween and then make the coolest costume herself. Every birthday was a celebration with a handmade birthday cake and party with a million friends from school. On Christmas, we sometimes took hot chocolate and sandwiches up the tramway and played in the snow. Summer vacation always meant a long road trip to some exciting new place. Whatever chaos was going on with my mother, and between her and my father, they kept it well hidden. My family was different than others because they made me feel loved, safe, and important.

In my teen years, I can recall a handful of incidents that must have been the result of my mother's DID. I can remember my mother grounding me for something I had done, only to have her ask me why I was home a while later. I also know her opinion of my father changed from hour to hour.

Aside from these isolated incidents, she was just a normal mom.

When I went away to college, I know things got difficult for my family. It was difficult on my mother. When my parents arrived at my college to move me into my dorms, I thought for sure they'd never leave me. My mother was horrified to learn I had been placed in an "apartment" with four boys on one side and four girls on the other. She was sure I'd be raped. Excited at being on my own and being that close to boys, there was no way I was leaving. Although I only stayed at college that first semester, I spoke with my mother on the phone every day. She also sent me care packages of home-made cookies.

At college I started hearing bits and pieces of discord at home and did not really know what was going on. I don't remember when I found out about her first suicide attempt or diagnosis. I don't remember who told me. After moving back home, I began to learn more about my mother's diagnosis and therapy. I participated in a few counseling sessions and remember driving with my father to the Los Angeles area to visit her in a treatment center. Between the issues my mother had with her brain tumor, her DID, and depression, I just remember my mother spending a lot of time in bed during the years that followed. As a selfish twenty-something, I feel I let my mother down during this time. I didn't lavish her with the attention she so generously had given me. I should have been a better daughter.

During my mother's early years of therapy, I can recall participating in the oddest event of my life.

I attended a birthday party for one of my mother's alters. It was a young boy; I think it was Joe. My mother invited several guests. There was a cake. I brought a gift.

The most frightening event in my life was when my mother tried to overdose on prescription medications. I was in the middle of a professional internship and spoke with my father in the parking lot of the facility during lunch. I hadn't heard from my mother in a few days, which usually meant she was depressed again. I kept calling the house, and my father finally answered. He didn't want to tell me at first, but after prodding, I learned my mother had taken two bottles of pills. My father thought she would be fine and would just "sleep it off." Something about that just didn't feel right.

Though he did not want to call the paramedics, I thought about it and felt really conflicted. After consulting with my husband and staff at the facility, I called Janet, my mother's therapist at the time, and 911. Later that night, I talked with my father on the phone and realized he was very upset over what I had done. My mother also called and left me a voicemail that was very cruel. In my heart I know I did the right thing. I also know my father did what he thought was the right thing. Thank God my mother survived. I went to see my mother the next day, and she apologized for the message. It was not really my mom that said those mean things; it was one of her alters.

I believe my relationship with my mother is closer now than ever. As a new mother, she is the first resource I look to when I have questions or worries. I miss her now that she has moved away, but in many ways, it helped me to appreciate her more. I feel that I, too, am a resource to my mother. There are many occasions where she feels frustrated about her disorder and wants to "just get over it." Sometimes she is in tears when she calls. I try to help focus on the things she can control and let go of the ones she can't. Most importantly, I always try to remind my mother how strong and courageous she is. To have overcome the hand she has been dealt is a miracle. She gave me the strength to become the woman and mother I am today. My mother is my hero.

Christy:

When I was in junior high school, my mom was going through many personal issues. She was depressed, suicidal, and finding out that she had multiple personalities because of an extremely difficult childhood. My parents kept me in the dark about a lot of it because they did not think I would understand or did not want me dealing with the information due to my age. We went to family counseling often. I did not want to talk about it with a stranger; I had close friends I confided in. My older sister was almost done with high school and not around much.

One day my mom and I were watching television in the living room and she asked, "Do you know who I am?" I said, "You're my mom." Mom said her name was Fran, and she was the personality that took care of me. My mom also had a personality that was a teenage girl; she liked to shop, eat out, and have fun with me.

I began to better understand what all she went through as a child and what caused her to have a dissociative disorder. I was happy that she survived it all and was able to raise two healthy children and have a successful marriage.

My mom is a lot better today; she has had a great deal of counseling to work through what she has experienced. She still has tough times when new memories come out, but she has a great support system with people who know and understand her. I would be lost without her. She is my best friend. She is an amazing woman who has dealt with adversity and wants to share her story to help others.

Chapter 21

Blessings

I feel like I am the luckiest person on earth. I have been allowed to start my life over again. Recently, we moved from the hot desert to the cool, green paradise of northwestern Washington State. I have gone from a chronically depressed person to a calm, relaxed, and overall happy individual. Not only is my hard work in therapy responsible for my overall improved mental health, I cannot ignore my spiritual reality—how God has blessed me in so many ways.

If you are a non-believer, you may look at my pain-filled life and wonder how I can dare say that I am lucky. You may say, "Look at all your pain and suffering! What are you thinking?" I can say with complete confidence that God has had his hand on me. He has guided me my whole life. The evidence in my belief is that I am still alive after everything I've gone through; I'm still here to share my life's journey with others.

For many years I tried to do everything myself, where my healing was concerned. Having a life so out of control, it is understandable that I felt the need to control everything. On some level, I must have thought this would keep me safe. I had to be in complete control of everything and everyone around me. Eventually, I had to admit to myself that my way was not working. I stopped one day and prayed to God. I said, "God, you know what is right for me. You created me and have a plan. Please, God, show me the way." And he did. Looking back, I can see so many areas where his guidance was evident. He put Robert in my path. He steered me toward helpful therapists. He helped me pick myself up after being down and out from physical and mental illnesses. I believe God also steered Robert and I to Washington, where we are so happy. I am no longer angry and driven to control everyone; now God is in control. I know that he will provide us with whatever we need in our lives.

With all of this being said, I believe that God also gave us a brain and free will to make any decisions we choose. I believe you can look at your adversities in life and use them as a learning tool. You can help others with the tools you discover. However horrible and painful my past was, it also made me a very caring and loving person who is sensitive of others' needs. I feel I can make a difference in this world, rather than just being all about my abused life.

My mindset is a choice, a decision, to not let the horrible things in life control me and to move forward with my life. The past is over. I survived for a reason. Now I want to discover what that reason is. I cannot do this if I remain a victim. Some people use their bad childhood experiences as a reason to disconnect by abusing drugs or to become addicted to alcohol. Worse, they use it to abuse others. Some seek abusive relationships. These people refuse to go forward in life for whatever the reason. I just know that I can't live a happy and fulfilling life by wearing my past like a coat for all to see and pity.

I am not damaged goods. I am not less of a person because of my abuse. I am responsible to steer my life, to pray, and to turn over in prayer all of my hurts and questions. My life is a decision. I choose to live life with God's guidance. There was so much that I did not have control of in my young life, and this is all the more reason to grab the proverbial horse reins and steer on, making good, life-affirming choices whenever I can. I never thought I could live near the ocean, and yet here I am just a block away.

Today my life is different than it has ever been. I have the freedom to pursue my interests and hobbies. Robert works about three days a week, so he is always home with me at night. My relationship with Robert is good and wonderfully comfortable. He understands me, and I understand him. We enjoy being together, whether we are reading the paper in the morning or going for a walk together. Robert still allows me to control when we have sex so that if I'm not in a good place inside, I don't even consider it. When I'm feeling altogether within myself, then that is the time we can be intimate together. In the new year, I plan to spend more time at the gym, and I might get a part-time job. I love to go on long walks and want to start bike riding when the snow clears.

I no longer have children at home to care for, but I have an excellent relationship with my daughters. I love them both very much. They make me so proud. Of course, I talk to both of them and my baby grand-daughter every couple of days. I also help Lorie with any medical issues that come up with her new daughter. I love that. Lorie and her husband, Dave, are wonderful parents. Christy and Lorie have turned out to be strong, intelligent, and caring women. I tried to instill in them a sense of independence, and I think that has helped both of them to control their own destinies. Both Lorie and Christy are in happy marriages. Both girls have graduated from college and have jobs that contribute to society. They both seem happy with their lives. I know for sure that I love being part of their lives.

I am not shameful or embarrassed by my DID diagnosis any more. I appreciate the fact that the alters came to protect me when I was a child trying to deal with horrendous abuse. They took the memories away and hid them from me. If I had to deal with all of the abuse, plus all of the memories of abuse on a daily basis as a child, I know that I would not have survived. The alters were there to protect me. That was, and is, a tremendous gift. I honor the alters for doing that for me. The most important thing about my life is that I have finally accepted my DID diagnosis, and like I said, I will always honor it.

As you can see, I have chosen to keep some of my alters. I have kept the whole, complete personalities, but I integrate the fragments. The personalities I have chosen to keep all have a function, and they help me to live my life more comfortably. As the original core personality, Dauna, I am the boss and keep all of the other personalities in line ... most of the time.

I have been asked how my disability affects my working life. I find that when a new alter comes to me, it is difficult to focus on anything else. I hear voices inside my head, and I feel sad for a while. I could not concentrate on a stressful nursing job right now. I might be able to do a less stressful job part time now, but I will just have to see how that goes. The main concern I have about working as a nurse is the fear of harming a patient due to my inability to concentrate. For a period of time during and after being diagnosed with DID, it is difficult to work. This is a time of exploration of one's self, but after a time, it may be possible. I have found that people with DID are intelligent and creative. They frequently go into professions where they help people. In order to develop DID in the first place, you must first possess the intelligence to discover this way to protect yourself from devastating abuse as a child. I also think that people with DID are sensitive to another's emotional state. They can sense a sadness or distress in someone when it is hidden from view.

I do not see a psychologist on a regular basis. I know that I will always need someone to call in a crisis situation. I have gone full-circle as far as therapy goes. I started in talk therapy and moved into EMDR, and then Lifespan Integration Therapy. I think all of the different therapy styles had their place in helping me. EMDR helped take the pain away from the memories that I have explored. Lifespan Integration taught me how to deal with an alter and how to integrate the fragments that just carry one memory. All of this therapy has helped me to understand myself and my diagnosis better. After moving to Washington, I found a new psychologist and tried cognitive therapy again. These sessions failed to help, and made me realize that cognitive therapy was not my solution. Everyone has an inner voice that helps them. Those of us with DID just have a few more inner voices that help us in different ways since we have more to deal with than the average person.

Although I don't want to trivialize our situation, I do think it's important to realize that having DID brings with it gifts as well as challenges; these gifts are insight and sensitivity into ourselves and others. DID survivors also have the strength to triumph over a lot in our lives. I have had suicidal feelings to overcome all of my life, for example. The difference is that these feelings have not come to me for a while now. I finally realized that if I commit suicide, my father wins. I do not want my father to cause the end of my life. I want to prove to myself and everyone else that I win. I have been able to recover from what was done to me. I have stopped the cycle of abuse in my generation. I have stopped the cycle of addiction in my family, and I have survived! I have not recovered on my own though; God has been with me and guided me throughout my life.

I want everyone that has been abused by someone in their childhood to know that you can get past it. Having DID is not the end of the world; it's the beginning of your new life. DID allows the victim of exceptional abuse the ability to "forget" the abuse and continue living. Without it, I may have gone crazy as a teen and spent my life in a psychiatric hospital. Maybe you are a clinician and are treating a DID survivor, or you are a survivor, or the loved one of a survivor. Whatever your relationship to this amazing and complicated diagnosis is, my hope in writing this was to further my own healing process and to guide other survivors on their own healing journey. Mostly, I want survivors to know that healing is possible and to remind them they are not alone.

Tips for living with DID

1. Keep a pad of paper next to your bed so you can write down your memories when they come out as nightmares in the middle of the night. Keep a drawing pad and crayons next to your bed so that if a child alter emerges during the night, they will be able to draw their memory.

2. Make a map of the inside of you where your alters are. Are there rooms for each alter, or are all of them in the same big room? How do they see outside of you? In my system, each of my alters has their own room, and they share a large living room. In the living room, there is a large screen where the alters can see outside of me. It is like a theater. I have read about a person with DID who has a system like riders on a bus, and whoever is driving the bus is in charge.

3. As a new alter emerges, write down their names and ages. Also, write down a little bit about their memories. It is also helpful if you write a description of each alter: male, female, red hair, blond hair, etc.

4. Have family meetings with your alters daily. When I have a family meeting with my alters, I lay on my bed with my eyes closed. Hopefully you can find a quiet place in which to have your meeting. I visualize each alter and speak to each of them individually. I ask if anyone is having a problem; if so, I ask that alter to speak to me and the other alters. Sometimes an alter just wants to be heard. If you plan to make a serious change, be sure to consult with your alters, otherwise they will sabotage you and your plans. I have also found that if I

do not have an internal meeting every day or two, my alters' voices will get louder and louder until I cannot function.

5. Keep your meds locked up and give the key to a trusted companion. There have been times when a new alter will emerge with suicidal thoughts. If your meds are under lock and key, you will be a lot safer.

6. Believe that the abuse did happen to you and that you're not crazy; you just have DID. This is a hard one. Psychologists and therapists do not just throw DID diagnoses around. They are very sure that is what you have, or they would not give you that diagnosis.

7. One way you can know if a memory is real is that it will come to you complete: the time of year, the temperature in the room, sounds that you heard at the time, your age, etc.

8. Find someone you can trust to confide in. Allow this person to help you know when your thinking is faulty. Sometimes we can be a bit paranoid. Sometimes we may just misjudge a person. It always helps to have someone you can talk to about your situation.

9. Take your psych. drugs exactly as they have been prescribed. Don't stop taking them just because you feel better. Don't take more because you feel you aren't getting well fast enough.

10. Last, but not least, pray to God to be with you, support you, and protect you. God has been my salvation. I would never be where I am today without the love and support I receive through prayer.

A person can go through so much adversity in life and come out on the other side as a survivor instead of a victim. It is all in the way you look at your life. You can have a positive attitude or a defeated, negative one. You can look at your adversity as a learning experience.

I am happy with the way I am now. I have a gentle, loving spirit. I would not want to change that about myself. If my childhood had been different, then I would be a different person today as well. I believe I can make a difference in this world. I already have made a difference in the world by giving birth to and raising two lovely daughters. I have also made a difference in people's lives throughout my years as a nurse. Please stop and take a look at your life. Your parents might have hurt you in your childhood, but you are in control of your future.

Endnotes

Endnotes

1. Hydrocephalus is a condition where the normal drainage of cerebrospinal fluid (CSF) in the brain is blocked in some way. Neurosurgeons classify hydrocephalus according to when the condition was developed (congenormal or acquired), and whether it was caused by a re absorption problem or a blockage somewhere within the ventricles (communicating or non-communicating). Communicating means the ventricles of the brain *communicate,* or pass along the CSF to the surface of the brain. The obstruction of CSF flow occurs not within the ventricles, but within the subarachnoid spaces of the brain. Communicating hydrocephalus can also be the result of a meningeal inflammation, such as an infection, or by blood or tumor cells in the subarachnoid spaces. Taken from, Chuck

Toporeck and Kellie Robinson. *Hydrocephalus: A Guide for patients, Families, & Friends.* 1999.

2. Hydrocephalus is a condition where the normal drainage of cerebrospinal fluid (CSF) in the brain is blocked in some way. Neurosurgeons classify hydrocephalus according to when the condition was developed (congenormal or acquired), and whether it was caused by a re absorption problem or a blockage somewhere within the ventricles (communicating or non-communicating). Communicating means the ventricles of the brain *communicate,* or pass along the CSF to the surface of the brain. The obstruction of CSF flow occurs not within the ventricles, but within the subarachnoid spaces of the brain. Communicating hydrocephalus can also be the result of a meningeal inflammation, such as an infection, or by blood or tumor cells in the subarachnoid spaces. Taken from, Chuck Toporeck and Kellie Robinson. *Hydrocephalus: A Guide for patients, Families, & Friends.* 1999.

3. Dissociation is the state in which a person becomes separated from reality. Dissociative Identity Disorder (DID), sometimes referred to as Multiple Personality Disorder (MPD), is a disorder involving a disturbance of identity in which two or more separate and distinct personality states (or identities) control the individual's behavior at different times. When under the control of one identity, the person is usually unable to remember some of the events that occurred while other personality was in control. The different identities are referred to as "alters." Alters may have experienced a distinct

personal history, self-image, and identity, including a separate name, as well as age. At least two of these personalities recurrently take control of the person's behavior. Multiplicity simply put by the majority of multiples is about hiding, pain, and survival no more, no less. It is a desperate completely creative and wonderful survival mechanism for the child who endures repeated abuse mentally, emotionally and physically it may be their only escape. Dissociation is a common defense mechanism against childhood abuse, there is no adult onset of multiple personality. Only children have the flexibility to fracture off from the "core" personality and escape the traumatic and painful memory. The common belief among most professionals is the personality splintered or fractured before the age of five. Alejandra Swartz. *Dissociative Identity Disorder.* AllPsych Journal. December 10, 2001.

4. Eye Movement Desensitization and Reprocessing (EMDR) is a comprehensive, integrative psychotherapy approach. It contains elements of many effective psychotherapies in structured protocols that are designed to maximize treatment effects. These include psychodynamic, cognitive behavioral, interpersonal, experiential, and body-centered therapies. http://www.emdr.com/briefdes.htm

5. Lifespan Integration is a new therapeutic technique which was developed by Peggy Pace beginning in 2002. Pace originally designed Lifespan Integration [LI] for treating adults who experi-

enced abuse or neglect in their childhoods. Since then, LI has been found to be effective with many different client populations and with all age groups. Lifespan Integration is now being successfully used by therapists in the United States, Canada, France, Spain, Sweden, Switzerland, and the United Kingdom. LI has been found to be extremely effective in the treatment of anxiety disorders, posttraumatic stress disorder, attachment disorders, eating disorders, somatic disorders, and dissociative disorders. http://www.lifespanintegration.com

6. Lumbar laminectomy is a surgical procedure most often performed to treat leg pain related to herniated discs, spinal stenosis, and other related conditions ... Spondylolisthesis (the slipping of one vertebra onto another) also can lead to compression. The goal of a laminectomy is to relieve pressure on the spinal cord or spinal nerve by widening the spinal canal. This is done by removing or trimming the lamina (roof) of the vertebrae to create more space for the nerves. A surgeon may perform a laminectomy with or without fusing vertebrae or removing part of a disc. Various devices (like screws or rods) may be used to enhance the ability to obtain a solid fusion and support unstable areas of the spine. Vincent Traynelis MD. *Understanding Lumbar Pain and Anatomy.*

7. Wendy Maltz. *The Sexual Healing Journey: A Guide for Survivors of Sexual Trauma.* Revised Edition. Collins Living.

listen|imagine|view|experience

AUDIO BOOK DOWNLOAD INCLUDED WITH THIS BOOK!

In your hands you hold a complete digital entertainment package. Besides purchasing the paper version of this book, this book includes a free download of the audio version of this book. Simply use the code listed below when visiting our website. Once downloaded to your computer, you can listen to the book through your computer's speakers, burn it to an audio CD or save the file to your portable music device (such as Apple's popular iPod) and listen on the go!

How to get your free audio book digital download:

1. Visit www.tatepublishing.com and click on the e|LIVE logo on the home page.
2. Enter the following coupon code:
   c349-f24d-840c-7c1b-0a04-3a4d-9b72-99a1
3. Download the audio book from your e|LIVE digital locker and begin enjoying your new digital entertainment package today!